DO YOUR OWN PUBLIC RELATIONS!

A guide for small businesses, organizations and individuals

Michael R. Gearlds

North Star Press
Hope, Idaho

Printed in the United States of America

Do Your Own Public Relations / Michael R. Gearlds / illustrations by the author

Notice of Liability

Trademarks and other Intellectual Property

ISBN 1469981505

CHAPTER INDEX

YOU CAN DO IT!

If you're part of a business or organization that wants to be better known and better liked, then you need to start thinking in terms of *public relations*. The fact that you're reading this right now is a great start. You're on your way to the goal of achieving more positive public awareness.

There is no great mystery about what public relations is and how it's done. The costly services of a PR professional can be of great value, but most small offices already have the basic talent to produce quality news releases and deal with the media *on their own*.

Just keep in mind that PR materials should not be exercises in literary flair or wit, but instead should be brief, information-packed, simply written documents of real interest to the audience. The plain "nuts and bolts" approach of this book should have you producing successful news releases in a very short time.

HOW TO USE THIS BOOK:

DO YOUR OWN PUBLIC RELATIONS! is a guide to performing basic public relations activities with professional results. Years of education and work experience in PR, advertising, teaching, photography and journalism have been condensed into these pages. Anecdotes and unnecessary details have been left out.

The three chapters, *Writing a News Release, Formatting a News Release* and *Sending a News Release* are the core of this book: The tools you'll use to create your publicity materials. Journalists produce their stories in a unique style, which has evolved from the needs of editors, proofreaders and typesetters. It's a style that's clear, information-rich and easy to edit – and easy to learn.

WHAT IS PUBLIC RELATIONS?

Public relations is the practice of gaining and maintaining positive *public awareness, understanding and support* toward a person, business, organization, product or service. Most businesses and organizations need to send out information constantly. Good PR practice ensures that information is part of a coordinated, goals-directed effort.

These goals are accomplished by arranging *favorable publicity* – presenting newsworthy information to the mass media and general public, and creating special events of interest. If an information effort is successful, the media responds by publishing or broadcasting items with a positive slant, at no cost to you.

Public relations is different from advertising in that it is an *uncontrolled* use of the media. That is, the success of a public relations effort depends largely on the *cooperation* of the media to carry your message. Above all, your message must be *newsworthy* – of genuine interest and usefulness – in order to gain the attention of the media and result in published stories, broadcast air time and other exposure.

Successful public relations is a *management approach*, expressed in procedures and practices effectively communicated to the community to earn awareness and support.

AREAS OF PUBLIC RELATIONS

Public relations activities can be divided into three general specialty areas. In the course of your in-house PR effort, you probably will deal with all of them eventually.

- **Product** public relations uses PR methods to promote products and services.

- **Financial** public relations supplies information mainly to business and trade magazines, newspaper business sections and investors.

- **Crisis** public relations uses PR techniques to fight, and hopefully *reverse*, negative public opinion or bad publicity.

WHY BOTHER WITH PUBLIC RELATIONS?

The continued existence and growth of your organization largely depends on maintaining two basic conditions:

- **The public knows that you exist.**
- **The public has a favorable opinion of you.**

A straightforward but *costly* way to achieve the above is to create *advertising* materials and buy placements in publications or spots on radio or television. But effective public relations can create, enhance or change public awareness and opinion – in a subtly more effective way than advertising can achieve.

Why? Because most PR-based news and features are *virtually indistinguishable* from other news, and thus have a *"legitimacy"* with the public that advertising lacks. Most readers, listeners and viewers are unaware they are seeing a PR-based item.

The majority of stories in the media have PR origins. Journalists depend on news releases and other PR materials for story leads, and they appreciate good ones. Studies have shown that more than half of the material in newspapers, magazines and radio/TV news programs were based solely on news releases. In many cases, the reporters made few or no changes to the material submitted to them and the items ran *virtually unedited*. One clue to identify PR-based stories: There's no "byline" for the writer.

Heavy reliance by reporters on PR materials is called *"press release journalism."* Still, when you submit a newsworthy news release to the media, you're providing a valuable and time-saving tool to deliver useful information to their audience.

In a crisis, effective public relations actually can *avoid legal problems*. Full, truthful, timely disclosure via news releases can ensure your side is heard in a *crisis,* and can help create a *sympathetic public attitude* that resonates all the way into the legal system.

PUBLIC RELATIONS IS COST-EFFECTIVE

The *cost* of having a PR agency prepare a news release, including time spent in gathering data, writing, editing, photography and meetings, can be *more than $1,000!* This does not include costs associated with production and mailing/distribution

A successful news release can generate many column inches of print or minutes of air time. Directly *paying* for such coverage in the form of advertising would cost thousands of dollars. Consider the cost of a PR-generated half-page article in a local newspaper, perhaps with photos, if it instead was a print display ad of the same size.

MEDIUMS OF COMMUNICATION WITHIN A COMMUNITY

If you're contemplating a public relations effort, consider all the options you have in targeting your publicity. Broadcast and print media are good, but there are many ways to publicize your message:

- *Print, radio, TV and other paid advertising*
- *Company publications – newsletters, magazines, billing inserts*
- *Open houses and tours*
- *Public speaking by employees*
- *Exhibits and displays at fairs, malls and other public venues*
- *Annual reports*
- *Contributions to community welfare*
- *Sports team sponsorships*
- *Cultural leadership and donations*
- *Educational assistance and scholarships*
- *Charity work*
- *Community promotion and improvement*

Many of the activities above will have their own public relations arrangements, and your participation should be *included* in their news releases and other publicity efforts. In other cases, publicizing your involvement will be up to *you*. Ask about their PR plans up front.

METHODS OF COMMUNICATION

The way in which you get your information to the media can be as formal as a news release or as personal as a telephone call or luncheon. Most editors would prefer a well-done, brief news release, but sometimes a phone call is appropriate, especially if circumstances prohibit the lead time needed to write and distribute a news release.

Consider the following alternate and companion methods to news releases in the course of designing your public relations effort, and refer to Chapter 12 – Other Media-Contact Methods for a more detailed discussion of them:

Personal Contacts

Feel free to make calls to friends, friends of friends, business clients and others with whom you have a *personal relationship* and who have media contact and influence to call attention to news concerning your organization. Personal contact can precede or follow sending a news release, depending on circumstances.

News Conferences

This method is used for *big announcements*, especially if the information calls for the personal touch of a principal speaker, perhaps with displays and graphics. A brief news release should announce the event about a week in advance.

Press Previews

This is similar to a news conference, but applies specifically to product PR, where the media are given a chance to sample or view a product or service in advance of its general release to the public. A news release should precede the preview event. Consider a "nondisclosure agreement" with attending media if the product or service needs to be kept under wraps for the time being.

Press Luncheons

Arranging lunch dates with editors, reporters or columnists is a widely used and accepted method of media contact. Your news should be the center of discussion, but this is a low-key, no-pressure effort, with PR balanced by friendly conversation.

Staff Announcements

These are a special kind of news release, and are a key source of information for business editors and local publications. They can stand alone or accompany other materials. Chapter 7 covers this topic in detail.

Fact Sheets and Media Kits

These items should be used with a news release and should not stand alone. You can find out about fact sheets and media kits in Chapter 8.

Paid Advertising

Print and broadcast ads can carry your message in ways virtually indistinguishable from normal programs, articles or editorials, but the station or publisher usually will insist on a small disclaimer or notice of paid placement. The main drawback is cost, just like regular paid advertising.

ELEMENTS OF A PUBLIC RELATIONS CAMPAIGN:

Public relations work usually entails a lot more than just doing news releases. An agency typically offers a whole program of action to persuade the media and the public. This book will show how a small office can undertake a campaign, starting small and taking on more tasks as staffers gain PR experience and confidence.

Following is a chronology of a public-relations campaign.

1. *Identify goals and expectations*

2. *Define project budget*

3. *Determine public opinion and problem areas*

4. *Design PR campaign within budget*

5. *Implement PR campaign*

6. *Determine public opinion midway*

7. *Make changes in campaign and budget as needed*

8. *End campaign*

9. *Measure results*

10. *Plan next campaign*

SERVICES OFFERED BY PUBLIC RELATIONS SPECIALISTS

In the course of a full-blown public relations campaign, PR professionals will do much more than write and mail news releases. Sometimes they will have to contract out for some of the following services and pass the cost on to their clients with a surcharge.

- **News Releases, Staff Announcements, Fact Sheets, Media Kits**
  These are the "bread and butter" of public relations. Basic, necessary tasks.

- **Feature Articles**
  Human-interest stories and consumer pieces, welcomed by small newspapers and industry publications with small staffs.

- **Special Events**
  Grand openings, parties, lunches, news conferences, contests, stunts.

- **Crisis Management**
  The PR agency acts as a consultant, spokesperson and buffer between the client and the media.

- **Theme Marketing**
  Public relations materials are produced to tie-in with an advertising campaign.

- **Speakers' Bureaus**

  The PR agency offers persons from your staff and other experts for talks and demonstrations. A list of speakers and topics is provided to groups such as civic clubs, schools and business organizations.

- **Market and Public-Opinion Research**

  Surveys are conducted and reports generated to identify public relations-related problems and to suggest a course of action.

- **Clipping Services**

  Monitors the media that receive your news releases and other materials to measure the success of your publicity effort and determine its effectiveness. Clipping services provide copies of PR-based articles, video and audiotapes, and produce summaries of air time and print space achieved.

- **Media Consultant**

  The PR agency advises your organization, using its valuable contacts and its knowledge and experience of the media.

Subsequent chapters will discuss various public relations services separately and assess the feasibility of a typical small office to attempt doing them in-house.

TAKE THE HIGH ROAD

Because public relations techniques are effective tools to get the public's attention and good opinion, they are used often – and often *misused*. PR professionals have earned a bad reputation in some quarters by spreading misinformation and hyperbole; promoting questionable causes; smearing individuals and organizations; and creating biased reports and studies. "Flack" is a pejorative term for a PR person, based on public perceptions of press agents practicing used-car salesman-type ethics.

But in reality, workers in the public relations industry rarely have the discretion to turn down clients based on character or moral issues. In this regard they are no different than lawyers, engineers, doctors, newspaper publishers, factory workers or anyone else who wants to keep their job and continue to make a living.

When you choose to do your own public relations, *you alone* are responsible for the quality of the product you produce and distribute, which should be honest, useful information. Appreciate that the media – particularly local media – quickly will grow wise to your methods if you habitually send them hype, lies and useless news releases.

Don't be a "flack." Keep your PR materials short and truthful. Produce and distribute them only when you think they will be of real interest and usefulness to the public.

CHAPTER 2
IN-HOUSE PUBLIC RELATIONS

WHAT A SMALL OFFICE/HOME OFFICE NEEDS

A reasonably competent individual or small office staff *already* has the in-house talent and equipment to perform most of the common public relations services discussed in Chapter 1. And remember this big advantage – you and your staff know your organization better than any outsider ever will.

Your personal computer and word processing software, along with a few reference materials and this book, are all you need to produce news releases and other PR materials. An Internet connection is almost mandatory, but you can manage without the Web if you're tech-challenged.

PERSONNEL

Writing, unfortunately, is one of those things that most people think they can do well – or well *enough* – but rarely can. Creating news releases is particularly touchy because you are sending them to journalists – people who produce thousands of correctly spelled words each day in proper grammatical order and filled with hundreds of verifiable facts.

A news release that is poorly written, inaccurate or contains misspelled words will make a bad impression on an editor or reporter, regardless of how newsworthy the subject.

Staff with secretarial or technical writing skills are good candidates to become your in-house public-relations pros. Executives and math-intensive types like programmers and engineers are usually poor candidates: They probably never had to become good writers in college and their position in the organization effectively eliminates frank editing of their work by subordinates.

It's also easy to step on toes by choosing the wrong person to proofread and edit your PR materials. The right person isn't necessarily the boss or the writer's immediate superior. Better yet, pick two proofreaders to spread the responsibility.

TRAINING

Sending the person responsible for writing your news releases to a basic journalism reporting class will do more to ensure the quality of your PR materials than anything else. Journalism style stresses accuracy and simplicity of composition, and "cub" reporters often have to *unlearn* writing habits acquired in college creative writing or radio/TV classes. A reporting class also will reinforce using the *Associated Press Stylebook* and the style and formatting conventions covered in Chapters 4 and 5.

In-house PR staff should have a comfortable proficiency in personal computer word processing programs, along with basic digital photograph image-editing skills, such as cropping and resizing for Internet distribution.

Staff also should understand computer file management, data-security procedures, such as regular backups, and the basics of how computer system files work. Attention to the fundamentals of data organization will do more to avoid headaches than anything else.

COMPUTER HARDWARE

Any writing task in this book can be accomplished with just a *typewriter,* but doing everything with a *personal computer* is a thousand times easier and produces professional results.

Additionally, you don't need a very powerful computer to do the type of word processing and image editing required for a small PR operation. A computer costing just a few hundred dollars will do just fine.

Better technology and lower prices keep "raising the bar" on what is considered a good basic system with potential for expansion, but it's really cutting-edge entertainment, like graphics-intensive games, that drives new personal computer technology, not small office business uses. Computers have offered the power to do fast word processing and handle digital images for at least a decade now. For the next few years, the setup described below is as good a recommendation as any.

The recommended **minimum** hardware setup is:

- A Windows-based *personal computer* with at least 4GB of memory, a hard drive with at least 750GB capacity and high-speed USB ports.

- A rewriteable *DVD drive* to back up your data and keep it safe, "out of the box." I also use an external hard drive as a "backup for my backup." I can't stress too strongly the importance of storing your data away from your PC, which will fail when you least expect it. Online backup services also are a good way to go.

- A *laser or inkjet printer* capable of six pages per minute, minimum.

- A plain-paper *fax machine.* For reasons covered in Chapter 6, "Sending a News Release," it is usually not a good idea to send your PR materials via fax, but some situations may call for the ability to send or receive a fax.

- A high-speed, dedicated *Internet connection*, or a separate dial-up telephone connection for modem Internet access that *doesn't disrupt* the normal flow of calls to your office.

COMPUTER SOFTWARE

Evolution produces winners in computer software, just as it does with living species, and today's clear winner in word processing is *Microsoft Word*, included in the *Microsoft Office* suite of programs. The free *OpenOffice* suite, is very similar to *MS Office* and can produce *Word-* and *Excel*-compatible documents.

Using other programs, even Microsoft's own *Works* suite, is asking for trouble. Stick with fully featured software that's universally used and recognized. You need to be confident that whoever receives your news release will be able to read it, print it and move text to their own programs. *Word* also has the advantage of being in such wide use, that it's much easier to find employees proficient in its features.

So throw away that office suite bundle that came free with your computer and stop considering that bargain software down at the office supply store. Microsoft *Office or OpenOffice* will give you an integrated collection of the business software "big three" – word processing, spreadsheet and database.

A big effort has been made to ensure these programs *work with each other*, with *common interfaces* and ease of moving information from one program to another, such as embedding a spreadsheet chart into a word processor text document.

But while office software suites have most of the tools needed for public relations work, you will almost certainly have to spend a little more to get the *digital image-editing functionality* you need for news releases.

Consider the latest versions of capable and popular programs like *Adobe Photoshop Elements* or *Corel Photo-Paint*. While these titles have many more features than you need to edit your public relations images, you can be assured they will have the tools you can't do without. When it comes to image editing, the *"$50 rule"* applies: If the program costs less than $50, it probably won't do what you need.

Virus-protection software to scan both incoming and outgoing e-mail messages and attachments is vital. I can't think of a better way to anger some newspaper editor than to send them a virus, albeit unwittingly.

Lastly, you will need to master some basic functions of your Internet e-mail program to create groups of e-mail addresses for your news releases, attach images, request read receipts and other conveniences.

And realize that although text files are small and quickly transmitted, when you attach *images* to your e-mails, it quickly balloons the size of the e-mail to the point where it may clog and tie-up someone's mail program. For this reason, you should learn to resize or resample your e-mailed digital images, as covered in Chapter 9.

REFERENCE MATERIALS

Essential to getting your spelling and facts right is keeping a small reference library handy in your writing area, literally at arm's reach. Chapter 16, "Reference Resources," lists a good basic reference collection, both printed and software-based.

Invest in a good hardbound dictionary, even though your word processor will have a spell-checker based on a supplied dictionary; a customizable dictionary to which you can add your own words; and a thesaurus. Surprisingly, not all English dictionaries spell all words the same way, so be careful what you buy for your own office.

The one *absolutely indispensable* item in your reference collection should be the *"Associated Press Stylebook and Briefing on Media Law."* This publication is your key to writing the way journalists do, and you should develop the habit of using it to look up *everything* in your news release to check for proper style and spelling.

Other reference materials can be had online or on DVDs or CDs, such as encyclopedias, atlases and various street map programs. Nearly all digital reference works feature "search engines" that greatly speed-up your information hunt, and using standard copy-and-paste functions, so it's easy to move blocks of information to your word processing documents with no time-consuming retyping needed.

Hint: Look for reference software that allows you to install its entire database on your hard drive, eliminating the need to connect to the company's Web site for information.

Finally, beware of information garnered from free Internet sites. The Web is full of opinions, bogus statistics and biased news masquerading as "facts." Try to cross- check your facts by consulting many sources, preferably from reliable operations.

STARTING OUT

The *news release* is a frequent and effective tool of the public relations professional. It is basically a *short news story* about *something of interest* to the audience.

A news release should be brief and to the point, and is a good way to begin learning PR writing. The next three chapters deal with the news value, style and format of a news release, and contain examples of news releases.

By the end of Chapter 5, "Formatting a News Release," you should be *ready* to write and format your *own one-page news release,* ready for distribution. Let's go!

CHAPTER 3

WHEN DO YOU NEED A NEWS RELEASE?

WHAT IS A NEWS RELEASE?

A *news release* is basically a *brief news story*, sent to the media in order to make them aware of a newsworthy development concerning your organization. News releases are the *primary tool* used by business to communicate with the media, which *relies heavily* on public relations material. *Legitimate* news releases save reporters a lot of work.

NEWS RELEASES ARE FREQUENTLY MISUSED

Public relations professionals and amateurs alike often are guilty of sending out news releases for no good reason and directing indiscriminate mass mailings to hundreds of newspapers, magazines, radio and TV stations, instead of intelligently and efficiently targeting their PR effort.

Most news releases end up deleted or in the wastebasket, because they contained no real news of interest or were sent to the wrong destination. You can earn an evil reputation, especially with local media, by repeatedly abusing information channels meant for legitimate news. You will save money, time and effort by making sensible judgments about the *"newsworthiness"* of your information.

NEWSWORTHINESS

The legitimacy of a news release, and its chances for acceptance by the media, depends on the elusive quality of *newsworthiness*.

Three main criteria are used by editors in selecting PR material for publication:

1. *Is it important to the audience?* It must be significant to the audience to be considered. Does the story have a local angle or impact?

2. *Is it timely?* It must be *news*, not something the editor had three days ago. Will it reach the readers early enough so they can take action, such as purchase tickets and find a baby-sitter.

3. *Is it accurate, truthful and complete?*

If your item meets *all three* criteria, it probably is newsworthy.

>   *And, if all else fails, are the people involved <u>interesting</u>?*

NEWSWORTHINESS MEANS MONEY TO THE MEDIA

Most media are fundamentally *vehicles to carry advertising*, not news or entertainment. The stories in a newspaper or programs on a TV channel are there to *wrap around* the *ads*, and would not exist without advertising.

Television programmers try to select programs the public will watch, not because popularity *itself* is a desirable goal, but because more popularity will gain *increased revenue* from *advertisers*. Print media operates in the same way, with advertising revenue being the *principal* income-producer, way ahead of subscriptions and newsstand sales.

The bottom line is that editors will select news release material for action primarily based on their perception of its importance and interest to an audience.

TYPICAL NEWSWORTHY TOPICS

While the following list is by no means complete, it will serve to give you a good general idea of what could be considered legitimate and newsworthy opportunities to produce a news release.

- Announcing an *important development*. You may have a breakthrough product or discovery. You may be adding employment to the local economy.

- New, unique or interesting services, products and situations.

- Your information is connected to a local or regional "hard news" story. This tie-in is called a *"news hook."*

- Your story offers a *local slant* on national news – a type of news hook. For example, your company produces desert survival gear used by the U.S. Army in a current conflict, or one of your employees is leaving to help out-of-state hurricane victims.

- You can offer *expert advice*, such as planning an exercise program or cleaning carpeting after flood damage.

- *Staff Announcements* – new personnel, promotions, professional recognition.

- Employee or company activities. Interesting stuff that's *linked* to your organization.

- Charitable activities and community service.

- Winning *awards*. Recognition via professional competitions always is newsworthy.

- Advance announcement of an *upcoming* event.

- Speaking engagements by company personnel.

- Your business or organization is new in the area.

- You're moving to a new location, expanding to another location or giving your reasons for closing an existing location.

- Attaining a milestone – $1 million in sales, 100 employees, 25 years in business, etc.

- *Merging* or changing the type of ownership – partnerships, consortiums, mergers – even teaming-up with another organization on a temporary or project-only basis.

- Doing business in foreign markets – particularly if it means more local employment.

- Increasing – or decreasing – your employment level.

- Changing your company's or organization's official name, logo or other branding.

- Celebrity appearances or involvement with your organization.

- Sponsoring an event or cultural activity.

- Filing for bankruptcy or reorganization.

- Going through a business or legal crisis.

- Involved in a legal matter reported by the media. Have your attorney advise you on the wisdom of using a news release about a lawsuit or criminal charge.

- Recovering or fully recovered from a crisis.

- Interesting or newsworthy people in your organization.

- Offering valuable and timely expert consumer advice.

- Coverage by the media. If you are the subject of a print or broadcast media story, this can be the basis of a news release.

- Offering info that can make money for the audience – real estate, investing, etc.

Several legitimate reasons to produce a news release may arise that combine to produce a golden opportunity. For example, you may be offering a new service that can be tied to the news in the form of expert consumer advice. A carpet cleaner who has recently acquired equipment or training to restore water-damaged rugs could be in the position to send a news release on "How to save your carpets" after a local flood.

Again, remember that most of the news and features you see broadcast and in print had origins in news releases. Even police departments and local governments use spokespersons and media specialists to supply information to the media. Reporters and editors rely on legitimate PR submittals for leads and to save time. Reporters also look to news releases when writing an advance story for an upcoming event, such as grand openings, speeches, meetings and news conferences.

News releases can provide an overview, details and statistics of an organization or event, which otherwise would require exhaustive and redundant legwork on the part of the media. In this manner, news releases also greatly help to reduce factual errors.

This is especially true if you use e-mail to send your news releases, because your media recipient on the other end can import large blocks of your text to their own story, cutting way down on the amount of retyping they have to do – and reducing "typos."

INAPPROPRIATE NEWS RELEASE TOPICS

As mentioned earlier, useless news releases clog the legitimate news channels to editors and reporters. Generally speaking, if your "news" is based solely on a profit motive or subjective opinion, it is *not* good material for a news release.

Consider the value of *waiting* to send a news release until you have real news to deliver. This will save time and effort for everyone involved, and will increase the impact of future legitimate news releases you produce.

Some *inappropriate topics* for news releases are:

- Sales and other retail promotions. While possibly of interest to consumers, these items should be handled through paid advertising.

- Editorial comments. Write a letter to the editor instead, but be prepared for negative fallout from a segment of the public that disagrees with you.

- Political involvement. If you wish to advance a political agenda – for a candidate or ballot proposition – do it through the public relations mechanisms of the political party or interest group directly involved. You can be effective without making new enemies.

- Your personal and business legal battles and gripes are usually of little interest to the media. In a situation where the media is interested, you can very well hurt your case by publishing information in the form of a news release.

- Staff junkets to conventions, usually in vacation spots like Las Vegas or Orlando.

- When you have idle staff time you want to fill by producing and sending news releases, regardless of their lack of news value.

- When you have nothing really new to report.

After you've determined your news really is news, the next step is researching, writing and formatting your news release according to standard and accepted journalism practice and getting it to the right people – as covered in the next three chapters.

CHAPTER 4
WRITING A NEWS RELEASE

JOURNALISM STYLE

This chapter deals with writing a news release in journalism style – a special way of writing that is simple and straightforward, and which puts a heavy emphasis on accuracy and brevity over creativity and displaying a large vocabulary.

Write your news releases like journalists write their news stories. This will make it familiar to them, easy to edit, and show that you know what you're doing.

The hallmarks of a well-written news story are inverted pyramid organization, summary lead, short sentences and paragraphs, verifiable facts in place of adjectives and adverbs, attributed facts and quotes, and overall brevity.

Journalism style was born of necessity, with reporters writing news stories on very short deadlines for readers that didn't have massive vocabularies or hours to spend on a single article. A formulaic style of writing was born, resulting in simply written, fact-filled copy.

Additionally, in a reaction to the "Yellow Journalism" newspaper excesses of the 19th and early 20th centuries, American laws clamped down on fictional or speculative stories, made-up quotes, subjective or emotional descriptions and doctored photographs. False news stories like this tended to be long, more like short fiction pieces than news stories.

Most importantly, the dual demands of hot-type printing plate production, which used cast lead alloy type and was not easy to change once a story was typeset, and very short deadlines for page composition, made it necessary to write news stories so that their overall length could be quickly cut to fit the space available without ruining them.

THE INVERTED PYRAMID

The answer was the "inverted pyramid" construction, in which all the *important* facts are at the beginning of the news story, followed by information that decreases in importance or interest as the reader continues toward the end. With the inverted pyramid, busy readers could obtain the meat of the story in the first few paragraphs – the *"lead"* – and then move on to another story if they weren't interested in more detail.

The inverted pyramid made editing and page composition much easier. In most cases, editors now could simply trim stories from the *bottom up* to fit the demands of space on the page, without losing the flow of the story or its organization.

Writing stories in short paragraphs also helped by allowing editors to cut length in smaller increments, without having to edit within huge paragraphs. Readers were presented with short, easier-to-read paragraphs, each centered on a single idea or quote.

Hot-lead typesetting still made composition tough: Old newspapers were full of little "fillers" at the bottom of stories, usually oddball facts or quotes. These bits were written and typeset during slow times and set aside, to be inserted between stories and ads to fill unwanted last-minute white space.

'INVERTED PYRAMID' STRUCTURE OF A NEWS STORY OR NEWS RELEASE

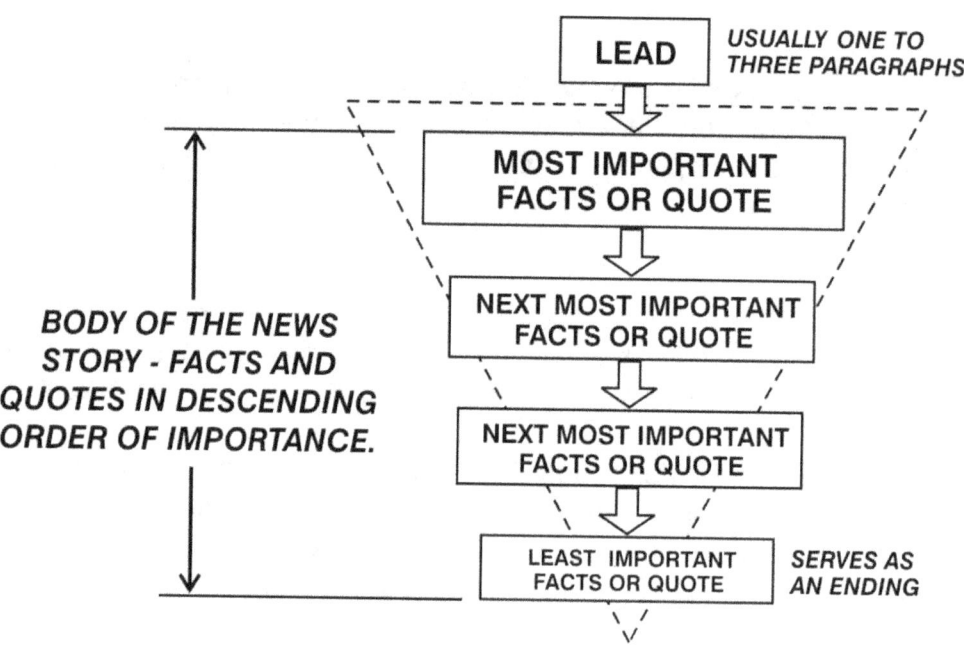

THE LEAD

The lead – pronounced *"leed"* – is simply the first one to three paragraphs of a news story. There are many types of leads, but the one best suited for a public relations news release is the *summary lead*, which puts all the important information of your story in the very beginning. There are other types of news leads, but the summary lead does the job well and is a good choice for writers new to journalism style.

The summary lead should answer the "five Ws" –

- *WHO?*
- *WHAT?*
- *WHERE?*
- *WHEN?*
- *WHY?*

Here is an example of a typical summary lead for a news release. In fact, because it gives all the significant news of the release up front, the rest of the release could be cut and just this lead would suffice as the whole story. Note the "dateline" at the very beginning.

```
TUCSON, Ariz. - Pete's Golf Cars is expanding to a third
location in the Green Valley area, at the northeast corner of
Renfrew and Oakdale roads, with a grand opening planned for
Saturday, Aug. 6.

The announcement was made Monday by company owner president
Peter M. Smith. He said the expansion will create nine full-
time jobs.

Smith said the expansion was triggered by high demand centered
around two new courses on the suburban south side.

The company is the city's largest golf car sales and service
organization, with annual gross revenues topping $10 million.
```

The news release could continue on at this point, with additional facts or quotes, but everything the reader really needs to knows already has been presented. By putting all the essential information up front in this manner, a good summary lead:

- **States clearly what the release is about**
- **Grabs the reader's interest**

THE ASSOCIATED PRESS STYLEBOOK

"The Associated Press Stylebook" should be your constant companion when preparing news releases. It's used by virtually every reporter in every newsroom. You shouldn't be writing news releases – or anything else – without one.

The book is organized in alphabetical order, like a dictionary, and is a veritable gold mine of information on proper names, abbreviations, spelling, usage, technical and business terms, punctuation and a lot more. It will answer questions you never knew you had.

For example, did you know "Muzak" is a trademarked proper noun for recorded background music and should be *capitalized*? Did you know "Space Age" is two words, both capitalized, and refers to an era that began Oct. 4, 1957? Do you know the difference between "arbitrate" and "mediate?" You will after reading the AP Stylebook.

There also are useful sections on media law and the Internet, as well as a guide to punctuation. Make sure you get the current edition, because the Stylebook changes on an ongoing basis, adding lots of news terms and sometimes even changing longstanding usage from previous editions. The book is readily available at larger bookstores and, of course, through Internet sellers.

When I taught college reporting classes, students were required to read two letter sections of the AP Stylebook each week, and then were given a closed-book quiz to test their real-world ability to apply the Stylebook's direction without having to open it for every little thing.

I have included those quizzes in Chapter 18. Try them after reading the letter chapters each quiz covers, then use your Stylebook to check how you did. This will reinforce using the book to check stuff you *thought* you knew.

JOURNALISM STYLE CHECKLIST

Use the following list to review your news release writing for conformity to the major stylistic, organizational and quality-control conventions of *newswriting*. The list is organized in the order you will be writing and proofing your news release.

It's also a useful exercise to compare the points in this list to a competent hard news story in your local paper. Notice how the reporter has incorporated journalism style and construction in ways the readers probably never would notice.

Refer to the next chapter, "Formatting Your News Release," for sample e-mail and hard copy news releases, as well as appearance elements such as fonts, margins, spacing, justification and exactly where to put headlines and contact information.

☑ **Subject matter and useful information, not style, makes news releases – and news stories – interesting.**

☑ Use the "*inverted pyramid*" structure. Leave the least-important information for the bottom of the release.

☑ *Summarize* your news release message with a one-line, uppercase *"headline"* at the top, before the main text. The headline should be a complete sentence, including a verb. Look at newspaper headlines for examples. See examples of news release headlines in Chapter 5 – Formatting a News Release.

☑ *Use a summary lead*, presenting all essential facts in the first one to three paragraphs. Try to get to the point in the very first sentence. If you can't write a short, simple sentence that summarizes your point, you need to do some rethinking about just what the point is. Think: How will this news affect the audience?

☑ Put the "*time element*" in the first or second paragraph. Tell the reader when this happened or when will it happen.

☑ Don't put *unknown names* in the first paragraph. Staff announcements are the exception.

☑ **Don't use TV news as your model for newswriting.** Television broadcast news has evolved into a combination of journalism and entertainment, with emotional impact often stressed over information and good writing.

☑ **Don't have someone write about a subject they know nothing about.** This will lead to errors you may not catch.

☑ **Do not begin the news release with a greeting or a person's name.** It's not a letter.

☑ **One-page length is preferable.** Two pages maximum. Length is not your friend.

☑ **Designate a contact person** for the news release and put their name, title, telephone number and e-mail address near the top, above the story and headline. Your contact should be someone close to the information, with the authority and judgment to answer questions. Eliminate middlemen as contacts – they'll just keep calling you to clarify things, or worse, plow ahead and get it all wrong.

☑ **Identify who made the staff announcement in the lead.**

☑ **Use a simple vocabulary.** Pick short words. Some readers won't understand long words – and even those long words with well-known meanings just make reading difficult and take up valuable space on the page.

☑ **Use the Associated Press Stylebook** for questions of spelling, abbreviation, etc. Note occasionally the Stylebook deviates from accepted dictionary entries. If you have to choose between the Stylebook and the dictionary, follow the Stylebook.

☑ For **general reference** use the **Webster's New World College Dictionary** from Wiley Publishing, Inc. This is the official dictionary of The Associated Press

☑ **Explain technical jargon in plain language.** Avoid technical terms or industry insider language. Rephrase jargon in "household terms" whenever you can. The simpler your message, the bigger the potential audience.

☑ **Describe, don't define.** Try to describe terms important to your news release in familiar language. Describe complicated or unfamiliar concepts using their everyday equivalents. For example, here's a good description of "kilowatt-hour":

```
A kilowatt-hour is about the amount of electricity it takes
to run a hand-held hair dryer for an hour.
```

☑ **Identify all persons completely.** This means first name – the *real* first name – middle initial, nickname, if applicable, last name and title.

```
Parts Manager James R. "Corky" Cook explained the situation.

Linda P. Coltrane, human resources director for the Green
Valley branch, said she was accepting applications.
```

Sometimes it may be appropriate to include the person's age or city of residence, especially if would help eliminate confusion or further distinguish that person from someone else. Straight news stories almost always include this extra information to avoid identification problems.

☑ **Don't refer to people by their first names.** Use a person's last name after providing a complete identification on first reference. Don't use the first name or a nickname. If two last names are in the story, such as husband and wife, use first and last name together. Other devices to make it clear who is speaking or referenced also work, such as "the elder Smith said" or "Smith looked at her husband."

☑ **Don't put honorifics before a name,** such as Mr., Mrs. and Ms.

☑ **Be accurate and truthful.** This is harder than you think.

☑ **Keep paragraphs to less than six typed lines.** Better yet, strive for *three lines*, tops. Use no more than three sentences in a paragraph. Aim for 50 to 60 words per paragraph, tops.

☑ **Keep sentences short, at under a dozen words.** Beware of overusing conjunctions like "and," "but" and "however" that will stretch your sentences. Try putting a period where you would usually put a comma. Short sentences make for short paragraphs.

☑ **Brush up on grammar and punctuation.** Don't assume you already know these things, especially as they apply to newswriting. Once you've mastered the correct use of periods, commas, semicolons, colons, dashes, hyphens and quotation marks, you'll know all you need about the punctuation that really matters.

☑ **Simple punctuation is best.** The AP Stylebook has an excellent section on punctuation. Some pretty awful twists on punctuation have entered into common use, such the *ellipsis* – those three periods that people keep using to "trail off" or show hesitation.

```
"I only wanted… a good education for my daughter," he sobbed.
```

The ellipsis and other junk like the *virgule* – that forward-slash that you often see on constructions like "and/or" – show lazy writing and deserve no place in your PR pieces – unless part of a proper name. Ditto for weird, little-used marks like brackets and double hyphens.

☑ **Don't use exclamation marks or question marks, even in quotes.** This looks amateurish. Let your readers add their own emphasis from context. Similarly, steer away from showing emphasis by using uppercase letters, except in headlines.

☑ **Don't imply or assign "states of mind."** They can, however, be suggested using quotes. Don't trust facial expressions, laughter or tears to indicate someone's mental state. Tears, for example, can be produced by sadness, happiness, pain – or *onions*.

☑ **Don't editorialize. Avoid hyperbole.** Reporters long ago learned to ignore it.

☑ **Leave out all adjectives of quality and degree and most adverbs, except in quotes.** Let the facts, numbers, dates, speak for themselves. *Show,* don't tell.

☑ **Cut the *"junk pronouns."*** Nearly every sentence containing "these," "that," "those" or "them" can be rewritten to be shorter and cleaner without sacrificing clarify.

☑ **Avoid the *"more than"* trap.** Give exact figures when they're available. Instead of "more than 20 homes," write "22 homes."

☑ **Avoid passive construction.** *Active* construction gives shorter, clearer sentences.

> *Passive:* Everything possible was done by company engineers to restore service.

> *Active:* Company engineers did everything they could to restore service.

☑ **Forget suspense, humor, fancy language and sarcasm.** Save it for the day when you get your own syndicated column.

☑ **Avoid "elegant variation."** Thinking of lots of ways to describe the same thing just makes your writing verbose and boring, like this sentence:

> When my books arrived, I took the hardbound texts from the package and placed the treasured volumes in my bookcase next to my other tomes.

☑ **Be aware of libel and invasion of privacy concepts.** Your news release is, in fact, a "publication" in the legal sense and is subject to laws governing publications. The ever-useful AP Stylebook has a "Briefing on Media Law" section that is a good basic guide to libel law, invasion of privacy and First Amendment Constitutional principles.

Chapter 14 – Legal Considerations also covers legal basics and expands some topics particularly relevant to public relations writing. When you communicate something to a third party, you have just broadcast or published that message – *so watch it.*

☑ **Avoid "sesquipedalianism"** - the excessive use of long words. Use "rain" instead of "precipitation," "use" instead of "utilize" and "fair" instead of "equitable."

☑ **Recognize redundancies.** We often *speak* this way, but shouldn't *write* this way. In the examples below, the words in parentheses are redundant.

(a distance of) 10 yards	(absolutely) essential	(future) plans
(as to) whether	cancel (out)	(very) unique
(baby) boy was born	(already) existing	might (possibly)
(first) began	(unintentional) mistake	protest (against)

☑ ***Watch out for commonly confused words.*** For example, check these words in the AP Stylebook for correct use:

adapt, adopt   awhile, a while
affect, effect   cement, concrete
allot, a lot   dual, duel
apparently, obviously   principal, principle
assure, ensure, insure

☑ ***Spelling errors leave a very bad impression.*** Always use word-processor spell-checkers, but don't rely on them. Fill up your own custom spell-checker dictionary.

☑ ***Be sure you know the difference between "that" and "which."*** Most people speak or write "which," when what they probably really mean is "that." Consider the following examples:

```
The lawnmower, which is broken, is in the garage.

The lawnmower that is broken is in the garage.
```

In the first sentence, the extra info is offered that the lawnmower is broken, but it's not important. The point is, the mower's in the garage, and by the way, it's broken. In the second sentence, you're saying that it's the broken lawnmower that's in the garage. This sentence would have been shorter and better if "that" hadn't been used at all.

```
The broken lawnmower is in the garage.
```

In general, use "which" only when you're conveying *nonessential information*, and surround that info with commas. The rule-of-thumb is "which with a hitch" – the comma is the "*hitch*."

☑ ***Eliminate parentheses.*** Using parentheses (like these) for asides, clarification, acronyms and other nonessential information is a lazy way of writing and should be avoided. Instead, use sentence construction with "which" and "that" to convey the same thing, only with a better reading flow.

☑ ***Watch out for junk words in common usage.*** The unfortunate English language is under constant assault by junk words that creep into common usage through sloppy writing and the failure of our schools to teach the basics. Following are some of the worst of the worst:

Alot – What people should write is, "a lot" to signify "many."
Author – This really isn't a verb. You *write* a book, not "author" it.
Orientate – Use "orient" instead.
Towards – The actual word is "toward."
Upwards – "Upward" is much preferred.

☑ **Proofread, proofread, PROOFREAD.** Spelling, punctuation, facts, story organization – *everything*. Use different systems to proofread, such as reading the text aloud or using the on-screen pointer or even a fingertip to march through your text.

Have other people proof the news release. No one can effectively proof their own work, so don't try to be both writer and proofreader. Anyone mentioned in the news release also should review it, if possible.

Proofread with a dirty mind; a litigious mind. Is there *any* way your writing could be interpreted as offensive, obscene or libelous? Could it prompt a legal suit, however ridiculous the grounds? Strenuous proofing could avert a date in court for you.

☑ **Eliminate unnecessary information.** Cut sentence length and redundant words. When you're finished editing your release, *find another 20 words to cut*.

QUOTES

Quotes are an essential feature of almost every good news story or news release. They add human interest and help relieve the text of unrelenting description and facts.

In newswriting, quotes should stand alone as separate paragraphs, no matter how short. In some cases, a bit of additional information can be added around the quote, such as:

```
"We're growing faster than expected," he said.

     or:

"We're growing faster than expected," he said, adding that a
new location was under consideration.
```

Use "*said*" or "*says*" when attributing quotes in news releases. Don't write that a person "laughed," "chortled," "chuckled," "snarled," "spat out," "insisted," "exclaimed," etc., when all you need to write is "said."

"Said" is the favored attribution method in straight news stories, and you'll see it used over and over again in a single piece. "Says" is more informal, and frequently is used in feature stories – personality profiles, "how-to" articles, humorous anecdotal stories and the like. Check out how your target publications do it.

Keep any quotes to a single speaker in any one paragraph. Don't combine back-and-forth conversational flow in a paragraph, as in the following *bad example*:

```
"We're growing faster than expected," Smith said. "It really
surprised us all," Jones added.
```

This is the correct way:

```
"We're growing faster than expected," Smith said.

"It really surprised us all," Jones added.
```

Avoid putting quotation marks around anything but an actual quote. Quote marks around other nouns, phrases, adjectives and adverbs imply *sarcasm or irony* – probably not the impression you're trying to make. Consider:

```
It is the "best" mousetrap available.
Ask about our "guarantee."
Enjoy "live" music while you dine.
```

Public relations writing differs from newswriting in that the PR writer can *make up quotes*, with the approval of the subject, presumably producing better, more interesting and informative verbiage than the persons being "quoted" could say.

CLEAR WRITING – SOME GUIDELINES

The following are concepts journalism students must master in their first semester reporting class. They're all applicable to news releases and writing in general.

- **Envision a general audience**
  Even with an audience of specialists, if you imagine an audience of *beginners*, your language will be clearer, less technical and convoluted. Imagine explaining a concept to an interested, but not too bright, relative.

- **Slow down the pace of information**
  Avoid a "dense pack" of facts – too much information stuffed into one paragraph, where two or three paragraphs would be clearer and more enjoyable.

- **Introduce new characters or difficult concepts one at a time**
  Explain the most basic terms, building on them to introduce progressively more difficult concepts. Introduce only one person or speaker per paragraph.

- **Recognize the value of repetition**
  Beware of *obvious* repetition – editors will cut it. But the heart of a story can be repeated in the lead, the ending or both.

- **Don't clutter leads with confusing statistics, technical information or bureaucratic names**
  Sneak up on the reader with complicated facts and difficult concepts. Don't assume readers know even common acronyms, like "EPA." Spell them out on first reference. The lead should be simple and straightforward – a narrative description, quote or one arresting statistic.

- **Use short, simple sentences**
  One clause – one idea. Short, simple *sentences* slow down the pace of information and help build short, simple *paragraphs*.

- **Remember that numbers can be numbing**
  Numbers turn readers off. Use word equivalents such as "half" or "nearly one in five" instead. Round large numbers up or down. For example change "$1,324,238" to "$1.3 million."

- **Translate jargon**
  Be very sure of your audience before you sling jargon about with abandon. The New York Times once defined the term "batting average" in a story about Ted Williams that was not in the sports section.

- **Find the microcosm**
  Find a specific, concrete example that represents the larger reality. The story will be clearer, more focused, more personal and easier to write.

- **Develop a chronology**
  When you develop a piece in chronological order, you invite the reader to enter a story and stick with it – with the implied promise that when the end is reached, they will have been rewarded. A chronology also creates order and organization for the writer when dealing with complicated or drawn-out topics.

- **Reward the reader**
  Alternate the important with the interesting. Follow statistics with an anecdote or useful advice. Inject humor or personal experience.

- **Communicate the impact**
  Why is what happened – or *will* happen – important? What does it mean to the audience? Is it likely to affect their family's health or finances?

- **Announce difficult concepts**
  Inform readers that upcoming information may be complicated and rough going: Don't make them feel stupid for not immediately grasping something. Such announcements ramp-up the concentration level of the reader and make harder information more tolerable.

- **Eliminate unnecessary information**
  The best way to deal with difficult information is to *leave it out of the story*. Make tough value judgments on the information you have collected. Sometimes, readers will understand more if given less.

  The result of such selectivity is a more precise, more readable story. If it turns out to be boring and difficult, at least it will be *brief*, boring and difficult.

- **Build "word pictures"**
  Exploit the impact of sensory perceptions – sounds, smells, textures, temperatures – to convey the sense of what it was like "to be there." This should add interest and readability to your news release without going over the edge into *creative writing*.

CAPTIONS

Captions are the text accompanying and explaining a photograph. All the images in your public relations submittals should have captions, written according to accepted journalistic standards. Photo captions should describe what's happening in the photo, and sometimes contain supportive information.

A caption can supplement a photo in five basic ways:

1. *Explain the action portrayed.*
2. *Identify people in the picture.*
3. *Indicate why the picture was taken and is being used – What's the news value?*
4. *Supply additional relevant information or point out interesting detail.*
5. *Give credit to the photographer or their organization supplying the image.*

Don't be surprised if a newspaper doesn't use your caption, and substitutes its own creation. This is not unusual, but don't let that stop you from writing and sending your own captions as standard operating procedure.

CAPTION STRUCTURE

The first line of the caption is called the "main descriptive sentence" and always should be written in the *present tense*. The main descriptive sentence "freezes the moment," just as the photo does. The rest of the caption can be in whatever tense makes sense.

The caption is, in form, content and intent, just like a basic news story. You can include a dateline and photo credit. PR-supplied images often are credited as "Courtesy photo" or "Photo courtesy (organization name)." For example:

```
HOPE, Idaho - Fernview Elementary School Principal
Mary Smith cuts the ribbon to formally open the
school's new library at a ceremony Monday. The
$300,000 library was built with funds from last
year's Educational Facility levy, and has more than
2,500 books. Photo courtesy Hope School District.
```

Try to keep your captions **less than 50 words long**, no matter how complex the subject matter. Write complete captions: Main descriptive sentence in present tense and the following caption body in whatever tense makes sense.

Avoid passive voice verbs. In the example above, Mary Smith cuts the ribbon, not "the ribbon *is cut by* Mary Smith." Adhere to AP style in all respects.

All of a busy reader's questions should be answered by the caption, in case they skip the story itself and only view the photograph and read the caption. Forget suspense or over-cleverness: Make your point in the first line of the caption.

THREE BASIC TYPES OF CAPTIONS

Normal captions; skeleton lines and namelines all fulfill the purpose of a caption, but differ fundamentally in how they do it. Normal captions are like little news stories; skeleton lines present a bare minimum of information, and namelines are just that – names, with maybe a little bit extra.

NORMAL CAPTIONS

Also called "full" captions, explain a picture, identify the people and things in it, and perform the five basic supplemental functions. They usually are composed in one to three sentences. This is the most typical type of caption that accompanies PR photographs. Most newspapers and some other types of publications use full captions with nearly every photograph. Include a dateline and photo credit with full captions.

Normal captions function perfectly well when linked to a story, but because they so thoroughly explain a photograph, they can allow the photo to run by itself, without a story, anywhere in the publication. For this reason, they're sometimes called "wild lines."

Normal captions are useful for public relations purposes because they give the media the option to run only the photo, without the story. This increases the chances the submitted photo will be published.

Normal captions often have little headlines of their own, called "overlines." These are a few well-chosen words to attract attention, reinforce the point of the photo or add humor or wit to an otherwise straightforward caption.

An overline can be a quote, a stock phrase or a single verb, adverb or adjective. Puns are common, but have been overused. Overlines can be all uppercase, for example:

```
ALL STEAMED UP

Hope, Idaho - Owner John Smith shows off his 1903
Hoyt-Clagwell steam tractor Saturday at Olde Farm Days
in Pioneer Park. The celebration of traditional
agriculture will continue today until 5 p.m.
Photo courtesy Mary Smith.
```

Not all publications like or accept overlines, so check out your target media to see if they use them.

SKELETON LINES

These short captions eliminate details, saving space and reading time, and are customarily used with pictures that have accompanying stories immediately adjacent to the photo. Overlines and datelines are not used with this type of caption.

Some publications use one line in skeleton captions, others, less commonly, two. Here's an example:

```
John Smith and his 1903 steam tractor.
```

NAMELINES

These very short captions are used on small "mug shots" of a subject's face. They usually give the person's name on one line and sometimes add a bit of elaboration on a second line, called an *expository line*. As with skeleton lines, omit overlines and datelines.

Often, only the last name is used on a mug shot if the person is well-known, or if they are covered heavily in the adjacent story. Mug shots with namelines often are used as a "layout breaker" in page composition. You may include a photo credit. Examples:

```
John Smith
```

or:

```
John Smith, steam tractor buff.
Photo courtesy Mary Smith.
```

WHEN IDENTIFICATION IS NEEDED

Photos of crowds, where no one is large enough or distinct enough to be recognized, can do without specific identification. But if someone is prominent, they must be identified. It not only is good journalistic practice, it makes the caption and photo more interesting and human.

Photos of remote action, such as a sailboat race, firefighters on the job or steeplejacks – where the photographer is isolated from contact with the subjects and faces are tiny, often can be excused from complete identification, but it's still a good idea to include names, if possible. Be patient and wait until you can approach your subject to get names, or obtain contact information and get identification later. E-mailing images to the people in them is a good way to get names, and is good public relations as well.

THE ASSOCIATED PRESS "10 TESTS OF A GOOD CAPTION"

1. Is it **complete**?

2. Does it **identify**, fully and completely?

3. Does it tell **when**?

4. Does it tell **where**?

5. Does it tell **what's** in the picture?

6. Are the **names spelled correctly**, with the proper names on the right people?

7. Is it **specific**?

8. Is it **easy to read**?

9. Have as many **adjectives** as possible **been removed**?

10. Does it **suggest another picture**?

THE CARDINAL RULE OF CAPTION WRITING

Never write a caption without seeing the photograph.

Yes, this actually happens – Usually under pressure of a deadline or when the writer is so sure they know what they're doing that they don't feel the need to double-check the actual image. Don't let this embarrassing blunder happen to you.

PLACING CAPTIONS

Chapter 5 – Formatting a News Release and Chapter 10 – Photographs, have information and examples of where and how to place or attach captions in public relations submittals with images.

Chapter 4: Writing a News Release

CHAPTER 5
<u>FORMATTING A NEWS RELEASE</u>

SO WHAT DOES A NEWS RELEASE LOOK LIKE?

The previous chapter dealt with how to write the body of a news release. Before sending it to the media, that text now must be formatted properly and supplemented by contact information, headlines and other features to make it complete.

WHY IS A CERTAIN FORMAT BETTER?

The organization and appearance of public relations materials evolved with newswriting: Both disciplines placed a premium on clarity, conciseness and ease of editing.

Whether you e-mail your news releases or use the old-school postal method, you will *greatly* increase your chances of success in generating publicity from your materials if they're formatted to professional standards.

Journalistic formatting has changed over the last decade because of the Web and its easier, faster way of exchanging information. Internet conventions on newswriting formats have carried-over to hard-copy documents, to the point where both electronic and printed news releases now share a fairly common appearance.

But important differences remain between how you should format your e-mailed public relations documents from what goes into an envelope. This chapter first will cover the formatting and appearance of an e-mailed news release. This is the recommended method to send PR materials.

If circumstances or personal preference lead you to send material via postal mail, the last part of the chapter shows how to format for printed news releases.

THE OLD WAYS ARE GONE

Back in the not-too-distant past, documents submitted to the media needed double- or even triple-spaced lines and wide margins to leave room for handwritten editing marks and notes.

Each typed or printed page contained a "slug line" with the name of the document, along with notations if the page was a continuation of a preceding one. If there was a following page, " (more) " was at the bottom of the page before. At the very end, "###" or a similar standard sign-off indicated the document ended and there were no more pages.

All these formatting conventions made it less likely pages would be lost or buried in a pile of paper while being handled in the newsroom.

If you are sending hard copy documents, you'll still need to learn and use some of the old formatting conventions, but e-mailed materials are handled differently and are much simpler to format.

COMPOSING E-MAILED PR DOCUMENTS

There are two ways to write your e-mailed news release – composing it within your e-mail program, such as Outlook Express – or using a word processor and copying the text to the body of the e-mail or sending the document files as an attachment.

Using e-mail programs to write documents other than brief messages is not a good idea. It's much easier to compose your news release and other public relations documents using a word processor, like Microsoft Word or OpenOffice Writer. These fully featured programs allow you to save the original documents in a universally recognized format for use as attachments, for archiving and for effortless cutting-and-pasting into e-mails.

PUT EVERYTHING IN THE BODY OF THE E-MAIL

This is the preferred method of sending your text. After completing your news release or other document in the word processor, select all, then copy and paste all into the body of the e-mail.

Putting everything in the body of the e-mail allows the recipient to view and work with it without having to open a separate attachment. This eliminates a bunch of mouse-clicking and fears that your attachment harbors a virus – making your PR submittal much more attractive and accessible.

Note: If you're sending more than one news release at a time, make them separate e-mails – each with its own subject line.

AS E-MAIL ATTACHMENTS

Sometimes, it will be necessary to include one or more attachments, but they should always accompany a news release that's in the body of the e-mail. You may even want to include an extra copy of the news release as a word processor file in the attachments.

Attachments will be needed if you're sending several documents at a time: Supporting materials, such as fact sheets, financial reports or staff profiles – or documents in the form of scanned images, like handwritten notes, old typewritten letters or newspaper clippings.

Attachments also may be in file formats other than word processor documents: PDFs, spreadsheets, PowerPoint presentations, digital movies and the like that cannot be placed in the body of the e-mail.

Photographs and other images in e-mailed news releases and other PR offering should always be attachments, not inserted into the body of the e-mail. The sheer size of modern digital images makes it clumsy to try to put them in the body. The recipient can see only a fraction of the picture and must go through another bunch of choices and mouse-clicks to view and save it properly.

FORMATTING E-MAILED NEWS RELEASES

Simplicity is the rule in presenting text in the body of your public relations e-mails. If your news generates interest in the media, they'll cut and paste your text for editing and pagination, or forward the whole e-mail to someone else in the organization to act on it.

Adhering to strict conventions on things like font choice and line spacing is less important for e-mails than hard copy documents – As long as the text is well-written and the media can retrieve the words and work with them.

Compare the "Formatting hard copy news releases" section later in this chapter to the format rules for e-mails to see how much easier the Internet has made the job of sending documents to the media.

Following are basic rules for formatting your e-mailed news release, in order from top to bottom of an e-mail program's new document screen:

INPUT BOXES ABOVE THE BODY OF THE E-MAIL:

- The "To" box should contain all the recipients to whom you're sending identical submittals. This is not only much easier than sending customized e-mails to each address, but might prompt some to act on your news before their competition – the other recipients plainly shown – gets the scoop.

- "Cc" and "Bcc:" should be left empty. To copy a public relations e-mail that was sent to the media to others in your own organization, forward it.

- The text in the "Subject" box should be simple, but descriptive – like the brief "slug" title that news stories use, plus notice that it's a news release. For example, a news release titled "ABC Manufacturing to expand local employment" could have a Subject box with the wording "ABC jobs news release" or "News release – ABC jobs."

THE BODY OF THE E-MAIL :

The actual news release story is preceded by several lines of information, giving the name of the business or organization sending the release; identifying the e-mail as a news release; telling when the information may be released to the public; and supplying extra information, such as listing attachments, photo caption text and helpful explanations to reduce confusion.

- These lines should be **bold**, to differentiate them from the news release text below. Bold is OK, because this part of the release won't be copied or edited by the media.

- Don't use fancy fonts. Stick to easy-to-read sans serif standards like Arial or Swiss. Use the same default font in both your word processor and e-mail programs. The same goes for font colors – Black is best. Anything else looks unprofessional.

- At the very top, identify your organization by name. This can be in the form of text, or a logo graphic built into your e-mail. Center or left-justify this line.

- Note: Your e-mail program may insist on double-spacing some lines on its own. Some experimenting may be needed to get the results you want when you paste text into an e-mail from a word processor. Check how differently text is handled if you choose "Rich Text (HTML)" or "Plain Text" under the "Format" menu.

- Double-space down below the name and alert your recipient in uppercase that the e-mail is a NEWS RELEASE. Use the same term if the message is a staff announcement.

- The first two lines should look something like this:

Pete's Golf Cars, Inc.

NEWS RELEASE

- From this point down, left-justify the rest of the bold-font information lines.

- Next, double-space down and show the *date* the news release is sent out. Spell out the month, then the day followed by a comma, and year. Follow AP Style for abbreviating month names longer than five letters. For example,

March 15, 2008

  or (for a month with a name longer than five letters)
Jan. 2, 2008

- Double-space down and put an uppercase "release line" immediately below the date. This formality tells the media they are free to release the information. The use of the term "immediate" is a good way to emphasize that the information in your release can be published or broadcast at any time. The usual text is:

FOR IMMEDIATE RELEASE

In some cases, the sender may want the information "embargoed" – that is, submitted to the media, but with a nondisclosure condition that it not be made public before a certain date. Here is a common embargo release line:

DO NOT RELEASE BEFORE MAY 15, 2009

The media may choose to ignore your embargo date of release, with the unspoken understanding that you will not be pleased and their action likely will negatively affect future relations with you.

Don't expect the media to sit on a really newsworthy story until your embargo date of release is reached. Also, they may or may not bother to contact you before breaching the embargo date. One way to avoid embargo problems is to approach a media operation prior to unveiling your specific information and work out a written, legal, *nondisclosure agreement* that they *must* honor.

- Again, double-space down and list your *principal* contact. Include name, telephone numbers and e-mail address. The contact person's title is OK, but optional. Other contacts can be at the end of the story. Try to put all of a contact's information on one line, as shown here:

Contact: Peter Smith, president, 555-555-1400, psmith@petesgolfcars.com

- Double-space down and put any special instructions or notifications in the form of an "editor's note" immediately under the contacts. This should be bold, except for text that is meant to be copied for cut-and-paste operations, like captions. For example:

Editor's note: Captions for attached JPEG images follow story.

- Double-space down from the contact line or editor's notes and summarize your message in a one-line, centered, uppercase, bold "headline." You can choose to write a two-part headline, called the "head" and "subhead," if extra explanation is needed. Separate the head and subhead by double spacing.

A headline should be a complete sentence, including a verb. Headline writing is a specialized form of journalism and is harder than it looks. Here are two examples:

PETE'S GOLF CARS EXPANDS TO THIRD LOCATION

or (using a *subhead*)

SOUTH SIDE PETE'S GOLF CARS OPENS

THIRD LOCATION CREATES NINE JOBS

- Double-space down from the headline and you're finally ready to place the text of your news release. Copy-and-paste from your word processor, or (harder) compose it within your e-mail program.

- Left-justify all text – even if that occasionally leaves a large blank space at the end of some lines where a large word was bumped down to the next line.

- Separate paragraphs by double-spacing.

- Don't use a first line indent on new paragraphs. See e-mail example at the end of this section.

- Single-space all lines within paragraphs. Double-spacing is not needed because no hard copy is likely to be printed and any text exchanging and editing that need to be done will be accomplished on the recipient's computer and network.

- Keep individual paragraphs to less than six typed lines. The preceding chapter's section on journalism style covers this topic more fully.

- Begin the *first paragraph* with an uppercase "dateline" that tells where the information originated. As with everything in print journalism, follow AP Style for datelines, as shown here:

    TUCSON, Ariz. – Construction on the nation's first pecan museum is set to begin Aug. 15 at a two-acre site on the city's south side. The facility will include several full-size pecan trees and a pecan products store.

- Show that the text of the news release ends – and doesn't continue in any way – by double-spacing below the last paragraph and typing three center-justified pound symbols. This is a holdover from the old, typed hard-copy days, but still serves at least two purposes – It leaves no doubt that the news release has reached its end, and it shows you know the conventions of newswriting. It looks like this:

                                    ###

- Double-space down from the ending pound symbols and include any extra information to complete the news release. This usually is a description of attachments and image captions, and the recipient should have been alerted by an editor's note near the top of the e-mail body that this information follows the release.

    Text that's intended to be directly used by the media – like the body of the release and captions – should be left-justified and not bold. Other types of information, such as file names and notes, should be bold.

For example:

Captions for attached JPEG images:

petersmith.jpg – Pete's Golf Cars, Inc. President Peter M. Smith.

petesgolfcarslogo2009.jpg – The new Pete's Golf Cars, Inc. logo.

On the following page is an example of what a properly formatted e-mail news release should look like on your computer screen, ready to go out to the media.

E-MAIL NEWS RELEASE EXAMPLE:

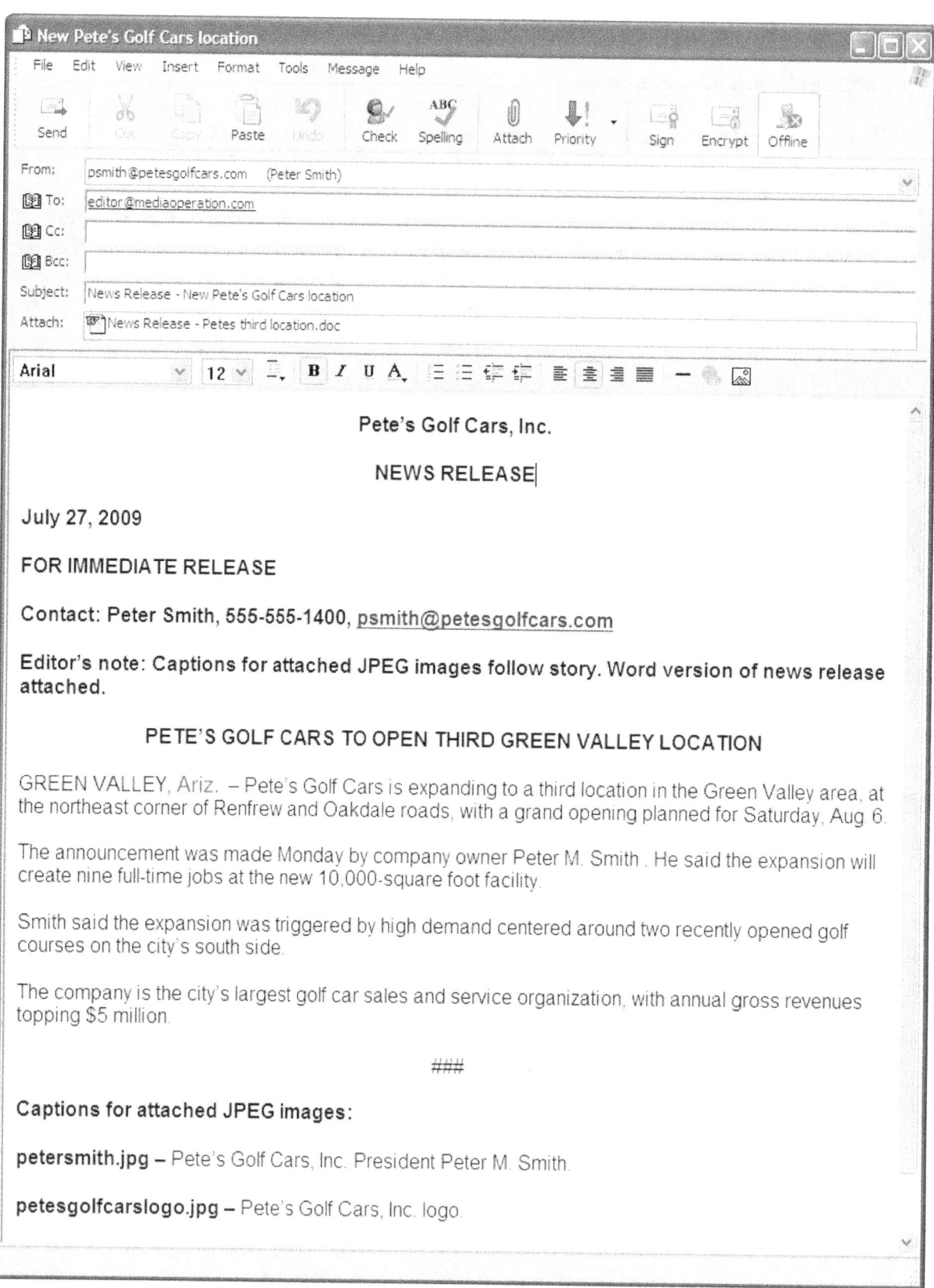

Chapter 5: Formatting

FORMATTING HARD COPY NEWS RELEASES

Most of the formatting conventions of e-mailed news releases apply to hard copy news releases, but some extra rules are in force – most are holdovers from the days before the Internet, word processors and e-mail.

Hard copy formatting rules still make sense, because they were developed to make reading and editing news stories and news releases easy and clear.

LAYOUT

The general structure of a hard copy news release looks a lot like its e-mail cousin, but with concessions made to allow room for edits, notes and corrections. Wide margins, double-spaced text and nonproportional, monospaced fonts are the rules here.

- At the very top, identify your organization by name, in bold characters. If you are printing on logo stationery, that graphic may substitute, as long as it's prominent and readable.

- Double-space down below the name, and in bold uppercase tell your recipient that the text that follows is a NEWS RELEASE.

- Next, double-space down again and show the date the release was sent out.

- Another double-space down, and type your bold, uppercase release line, usually "FOR IMMEDIATE RELEASE."

- Single-space down, and type the information for your principal contact in bold.

- Double-space down from the contact information, and place your editor's notes, if you need any.

- Triple-space down from the contact information or editors notes and type your news release headline in bold, uppercase, centered letters.

- Double-space down from the headline and begin the first paragraph of your news release.

From this point, the hard copy news release follows the structure and writing conventions covered in Chapter Four – Writing a News Release. The biggest difference from the e-mail version is the monospaced font and the use of double-spacing throughout the body text.

An example of a hard copy news release can be found at the end of this chapter, but first, a few words on choosing paper and ink.

PAPER

- Use **white paper**, unless your letterhead stationery normally is on colored stock. Even then, don't use your stock if its color, texture or pattern makes scaning text difficult. The tactics of using bright papers and unusual fonts will not make your release more noticeable to an editor or news director, but *will* greatly increase its chances of being thrown away, unread.

- Stick to letter-size paper. Don't use legal, executive, metric or other odd-size papers. You want to ensure your news release will fit in standard copiers, scanners, file folders – and, yes, shredders.

- Put the news release on your company or organization letterhead stationery. If the release is produced by a PR agency, avoid using their letterhead – The release should concern your organization, not serve as an ad for the PR consultant. No letterhead is preferable to a third-party letterhead.

- Print your release in *black*. If your letterhead is printed in color, that's OK, but print everything else on the page in black. Colored inks usually are harder to read, and may not photocopy or scan well.

FONT

- Use a 10- or 12-point "monospaced" font, similar to what most typewriters put out. Each character takes up the same amount of space, regardless of size. Avoid proportional or artsy fonts, which are harder to scan and edit, and can confuse optical character recognition – *OCR* – programs, which might produce errors in the scanned text.

- The best font choice for hard copy news releases is the old typewriter standby, Courier, shown below. Notice how the 10-point size is a bit small for easy reading and editing markup:

  ```
  Courier 10 point

  Courier 12 point
  ```

  The body text of this book is set in 12-point "Swiss 721 BT," also called "Helvetica," a proportional font that's unsuitable for printed news releases.

- With the exception of the headline and all the lines of information above it – as well as whatever information you include below the sign-off – don't use bold characters. Avoid italic and underlined characters totally. Weighting fonts in this manner is used to indicate stress or relative importance – but not in journalism writing. Leave it to the media to recognize what is important in your information. Similarly, avoid using all-uppercase text, except in the headline, acronyms and abbreviations.

HARD COPY FORMAT GUIDELINES

- Use 1-inch margins all around.

- Left-justify all text in the body of the release, with the exceptions of the centered headline(s) at the beginning and sign-off pound symbols at the end. Leave the right margin "ragged."

- Avoid full justification, which often inserts unusually wide spaces between words and sentences.

- Double-space all text in body of release. This gives editors room for questions, comments and corrections. Not too far in the past, newspaper reporters had to *triple-space* hard copy to make room for editing.

- Don't indent the first line to indicate a new paragraph.

- Add an extra space between paragraphs.

- Don't split paragraphs between pages. If the whole paragraph will not fit on a page, move it entirely to the next page.

- Don't hyphenate between lines. Keep compound words together on the same line, even if it means a lot of white space at the end of a line.

- If you need a following page, at the bottom center of the preceding page, put

```
(more)
```

On the second page – or third, or fourth, etc. – at the top left of that page put your business or organization name, followed below by the news release "slug" – a one- or two-word lowercase name of your news release.

Like the headline, the slug should summarize what the release is about. If your release is circulated in a media office or put into publication or broadcast, it probably will be known by its slug. A news release about Pete's Golf Cars expanding to a new location could be given the slug, "Pete's expansion."

The slug is followed by the page number header. A second page is called "add one"; a third page would be called "add two." For example, a second page of that news release would have this kind of two-line tag at the upper left:

```
Pete's Golf Cars, Inc.
pete's expansion – add one
```

- Use (more) at the bottom of each page preceding the last page. Remember that the *readability* of a news release is inversely proportional to its length: shorter is better.

- At the end of the release, sign-off in the center after double-spacing from last line with three pound symbols:

###

- Below the sign-off, put any additional information promised in the editor's note near the top of the news release. Typical items include a list of attachments, if any, and photograph captions.

- Staple everything together. Nothing should be loose.

- Attach artwork, illustrations and photos taped to letter-size paper and stapled with the rest of the release. Don't staple through the art or photo itself. Refer to Chapter 10 – Photographs, for methods to attach captions to hard copy images.

- Fact sheets should be stapled to the release. Some large items, such as brochures or catalogs, can be clipped or enclosed. Be prepared to have unstapled pieces lost.

On the following page is a reduced-size example of what a properly formatted, one-page hard copy news release should look like.

PRINTED NEWS RELEASE EXAMPLE:

Pete's Golf Cars, Inc.

NEWS RELEASE

July 27, 2009

FOR IMMEDIATE RELEASE
Contact: Peter Smith, 555-555-1400

Editor's note: Caption for attached 4x6 print photograph follows story and also is stapled to print.

PETE'S GOLF CARS TO OPEN THIRD GREEN VALLEY LOCATION

GREEN VALLEY, Ariz. — Pete's Golf Cars is expanding to a third location in the Green Valley area, at the northeast corner of Renfrew and Oakdale roads, with a grand opening planned for Saturday, Aug. 6.

The announcement was made Monday by company owner Peter M. Smith. He said the expansion will create nine full-time jobs at the new 10,000-square foot facility.

Smith said the expansion was triggered by high demand centered around two recently opened golf courses on the city's south side.

The company is the city's largest golf car sales and service organization, with annual gross revenues topping $5 million.

###

Caption for attached print photograph:

Pete's Golf Cars, Inc. President Peter M. Smith.

E-MAIL IS THE WAY TO GO

In the days before the Internet, public relations materials were submitted to newspapers and other media in hard copy form via mail, courier or in person. Some PR items still reach the media that way – things like thick, glossy press kits from professionals, or crude, typewritten announcements from amateurs.

But Internet e-mail has changed the way public relations is done. Newspapers, television and other destinations for your news releases prefer to get them as e-mail messages and attachments.

Even faxes are much less welcome than a well-composed e-mail. With faxing, you're using up your recipient's fax paper and ink and toner for stuff they never requested. Not a great way to get on someone's good graces.

Faxes still can be used in special circumstances: For example, when your item is a hard copy graphic and you don't have a scanner. Keep in mind, though, that even the best faxes lack the resolution and quality of e-mailed images. For public relations purposes, consider faxing as an outdated bridge technology between the old-style postal "snail mail" and today's e-mailing that should be avoided if at all possible.

Now, nearly everyone uses e-mail for their submittals to the media and no longer do editors and reporters have to sort through and open dozens of envelopes every day, discarding most of them. E-mails can be quickly viewed and, if of no interest, deleted.

E-mailed PR materials can be copied and inserted into a reporter's word processor document without laborious and error-prone retyping. This alone greatly increases your chances of the media accepting your news release and doing something with it.

Supporting documents, graphics and photographs can be attached in digital form, ready to use. Clickable e-mail addresses for your contacts and Internet links to relevant Web sites also are easy to include.

And e-mail news releases are much cheaper for everybody involved. The sender doesn't have to spend a small fortune on postage, envelopes, paper, photographic prints and the time needed to assemble multiple mailings of the same material.

On the receiving end, no printing usually is needed – documents and supporting items can be viewed, copied, used or discarded with no hard copies ever made.

ALTERNATIVE DELIVERY METHODS

One of the few acceptable alternatives to e-mailing PR material is to deliver it in person, which brings with it the possible advantage of personal contact and salesmanship. On the other hand, it uses much more time for everyone concerned, especially the busy media person who must put aside their work to meet with you and hear your pitch.

If your public relations submittal includes items that can't be e-mailed, such as a glossy, professional brochure or product sample, then by all means mail it, ship it or deliver the package in person.

TO ATTACH – OR NOT TO ATTACH?

Most news releases, staff announcements and other brief public relations submittals should be sent as text in the body of an e-mail, not as attachments. Photographs, graphics and other large, should be included as attachments.

The reason is that this type of e-mailed document is much easier to view and copy than opening separate attachments. Saving time and mouse-clicks on the receiving end can be a big bonus for your PR effort. Also, some recipients avoid opening attachments due to virus fears, or their network security setup may quarantine e-mails with attachments.

Just because your PR submittal is text in the body of the e-mail and not an attached document doesn't mean it has to be plain: Such e-mails can be created on custom, stationary-look backgrounds and feature logos, images and signatures. Just be careful not to compromise the cut-and-paste utility of putting your message in text form by making your recipient navigate around graphics embedded inside the text.

ATTACHMENTS

Almost without exception, any media operation can be expected to have some kind of high-speed broadband Internet service, so their computer systems won't be bogged-down by huge e-mails with attachments containing high-resolution images or other common types of large file formats, such as PDFs.

Refer to attachments in the body of the e-mail the same way you would reference attachments in a printed document. At the bottom of the page, include something like:

attachments:

> **johnsmith.jpg** – John Smith head shot, color
> **smithstore.jpg** – Smith & Sons storefront, color
> **smithstoreint.jpg** – Smith & Sons store interior, color

E-mail attachments also are flagged for the recipient by a symbol – usually a paperclip – and are listed in the "Attach:" box by filename and file size. But also giving your recipient an additional heads-up and description in the news release itself works better.

WHERE DO YOU SEND RELEASES?

- **Newspapers** – Local print media. In addition to hard news, papers run features and stories of interest to the community – business, travel, consumer news, local issues, events and profiles of area people.

- **Magazines** – An important medium for product news, feature stories and pictures. Magazines serve varied audiences: Local, state, national, trade, special interest, age groups, niche markets, etc.

- **Radio/Television** – Local broadcast news productions have the traditional mix of news and features seen in current-events magazines like *Time* and *Newsweek*. Radio/TV news departments typically have smaller reporting staffs than newspapers and often lean on print media and public relations-origin information for story leads.

- **Non-media** – Destinations can include clubs and organizations, newsletters, public and private schools, consumer groups, customers, chambers of commerce – even friends and family. Anyone who might be interested in your PR submittal and is in a position to pass it on to an audience.

- **Newspaper feature, photo and news syndicates** – If you have information that's *really* newsworthy or useful, this is worth a try. Get contact information from their Web sites.

TO WHOM DO YOU SEND NEWS RELEASES?

The more knowledgeable you are about the structure and people of the media organization you're contacting, the better your chances of getting the attention of the right person in a position to act on your information.

Avoid sending your public relations submittals to a general e-mail address. Try to find out who is the correct person in the organization to directly contact, along with their title, and get their e-mail information.

A good start on learning about a newspaper or magazine is to check out the "staff box," which typically is near the front of the publication, around a magazine's contents page or a newspaper's page 2.

The staff box usually will list only publishers, editors and other upper-echelon positions, along with general contact information – telephone numbers, along with e-mail, mailing and street addresses.

Don't mail your PR stuff to a plain street address or P.O. box without first trying to get the name and title of the person you want to reach. Put that information on the front of the envelope. For example:

Attention: Peter Cooper, business editor

If you are unable to find a specific person, direct your e-mails or postal mails to a generic department or title – whether it actually exists in the media organization or not – such as "business editor" or "sports department."

TYPICAL POSITIONS TO CONTACT

- **Editors** – usually the best person to reach in small media organizations, like weekly newspapers. Some publications will have several types of general editors, like "editorial director," "managing editor" or "assistant editor." Call to find out who is the best editor for your type of information.

- **Special editors** – such as news, features, business, sports, homes, city. This kind of hierarchy is typical for larger newspapers and publications.

- **News Directors** – a broadcast news title synonymous with "editor" in print media.

- **Reporters** – Certain reporters cover specific "beats," like education, business, etc.

- **Staff writers** – A more general kind of reporter that creates features in addition to hard news.

- **Publishers** – The person above the editor, at the top of the organization. Contact this person only as a last resort.

CREATING MEDIA LISTS

The contact information you collect from staff boxes, telephoning media organizations and other contact efforts will be organized in one or more "media lists."

You may need to create different media lists for various markets or types of public relations releases: A list that's proper for news releases may not be the same as one for staff announcements, or one that's good for local-interest submittals will be much smaller than one for national release.

Once upon a time, a media list was a typewritten or word processor document that was photocopied or printed onto mailing label stock. Labels also can be created from media list address documents and formatted to merge on various label or envelope stock.

Don't try to merge media contact names into "personalized" news releases with greetings like, "Dear Jack Adams." This looks amateurish, and won't help sell your information.

With the ascendancy of e-mail as the preferred way to send PR materials to the media, the old hardcopy/mail merge way of managing and printing media lists has been left behind. E-mail programs now let you easily create, update and use address lists for mass mailings at no cost. Former cost considerations for the printing, folding, envelopes and postage needed for dozens – or hundreds – of PR mailings now are largely a thing of the past.

Yet another reason to embrace e-mail as your public relations transmittal method of choice.

However, if your media list is small, or your materials are best sent in physical form, you will want to create and maintain a media list that is ready to print on labels or envelopes. Lists with a small number of contacts can be created and easily updated as graphics files with programs like Adobe Illustrator or CorelDraw, with the label edges shown as guidelines. A reduced-size example is shown below:

Jack Adams
News Director
KUUR-TV
1212 W. Pomegranite Road
Tucson, AZ 85701

Maureen Allen
Editor
ARIZONA COMMERCE NEWS
c/o Cactus University
50 N. Mountain Pass Way
Tucson, AZ 85701

Thom Caine
City Editor
TUCSON DAILY CHRONICLE
777 S. Lakeview Drive
Tucson, AZ 85701-1212

K.M. Gersen
Special Writer
COSMOPOLIS
Tucson Media Centre
1 N. Dalt Avenue
Tucson, AZ 85701

Cindy Hayne-Robinson
Southern Arizona Editor
SOUTHWEST JOURNAL
3348 E. Harvard St.
Tucson, AZ 85701

Ray Kramer
Program Manager
KSUP-AM Radio
Nedway Business Park, #14
400 S. Cotton Gin Road
Tucson, AZ 85701

Meredith Munro
News Editor
GOLF CAR WORLD
162 Beachcomber Road
San Luis Obispo, CA 91088

M. Ridolph
Editor
TUCSON BUSINESS UPDATE
2824 S. Vance Parkway
Tucson, AZ 85701

Julio Robles
Program Director
KMEQ-FM Radio
756 W. Business Circle,
Suite 200
Tucson, AZ 85701

Katherine Wu
News Director
KQWE-FM/KQWR-AM Radio
4679 E. 54th St.
Tucson, AZ 85701

Rainbow Zen
Editor and Publisher
Alternate Modes Magazine
1722A N. College Ave.
Tucson, AZ 85701

MAINTAIN YOUR MEDIA LIST

After you've created a media list, the work is not over. The list must be checked and updated periodically to keep up with changes at your target media operations. Constant change is the watchword in news organizations, with a sometimes-high degree of turnover in staff and editorial management.

Compare current publication staff boxes to your media list, to make sure you won't send something to someone who isn't there anymore or who has been shifted to a different position. For publications you haven't seen in a long time, check if they even still exist.

Set your e-mail default to always request a read receipt. Lots of people still won't do that mouse-click to let you know they've seen your e-mail, but if you regularly do not see a read receipt from a certain address, find out if that person still is with the organization.

If you regularly don't get a read receipt or inquiry from a media operation you think would be interested in your news, following up with a telephone call is good practice.

TIMING IS EVERYTHING

When you send your public relations material is important to gain maximum consideration by the media.

In nearly every case, send your information when you're ready to have it publicized. "For immediate release" is standard practice to place at the top of news releases and other PR submittals, as shown in Chapter 5, and lets the media know it's OK to proceed with running the info.

In certain situations, however, you may want to alert the media of your news and give them time to act on it, but are not ready to have it publicized to the public. To do this, you "embargo" your information by placing a *date of release* at the top, such as:

FOR RELEASE 5/20/2008

or:

DO NOT RELEASE BEFORE MAY 20

or:

HOLD UNTIL MAY 20

Unless your embargo date crosses into the next year, it is not necessary to include the year in your release line. If you use a numeral-and-slash format for the embargo date, such as "5/20/2008," then include the year.

ADVANCE NOTICE

An audience should be given about a week's notice of an event. *Long* advance notice means they're more likely to forget about it by the time it happens. *Short* notice makes it less likely they'll shift around plans in order to attend.

Some advance notice requirements are set by law, such as a certain number of days notice for public hearings and elections. The law also may require several notices be published in advance, and sets the days each notice must have before the proceeding.

For daily newspapers, 24 hours advance notice of an event, such a news conference, speech or grand opening, is the minimum. Better to give them two or three days, if possible, to weigh the value of your event and assign staff to cover it.

Broadcast media is more immediate, generally has less depth to its reporting and has shorter deadlines – as short as four to six hours before air time. Still, 24 hours advance notice is appropriate, if possible. Two or three days is better.

DEADLINES

Print and broadcast media operations are driven by deadlines. Some are short, such as a 5 p.m. deadline to make the next morning's newspaper. Others are longer, for productions reasons or to give time for the reporting staff to act on your information.

Other deadlines are made necessary by the needs of advertising placements or to give the public time reasonable time to react.

Most publications and broadcast programs are primarily vehicles for advertising and wouldn't exit without it. For that reason, page space and airtime for ads have precedence over most news – up the limit the audience will tolerate.

NEWSPAPER DEADLINES

Morning newspapers are put together the previous afternoon and evening, and 5 p.m. is a typical deadline for reporters to hand in their stories. Afternoon papers are composited from the previous afternoon to noon of the same day, and have late-morning deadlines at the latest.

Weekly newspapers usually have end of business hours deadlines on a certain day of the week, and you will have to check with each one individually for their requirements.

Newspapers with Sunday editions typically need information by Friday morning to be considered. Sunday papers are larger than the Monday-Saturday editions and newsroom staffs are smaller on Saturday, so your chances of a Sunday placement may be better because the newspaper needs more material for that day.

Mondays are normally light news days and, because much of the editorial staff was off on the weekend, editors have fewer stories to work with. For that reason, Monday is a good day to target for a PR submittal. Material should arrive at a newspaper the previous Friday or over the weekend to gain the attention of an editor Monday morning.

Midweek newspapers have lots of advertising, leaving less room for PR-origin stories. Public relations items submitted Monday through Wednesday may get less attention because they're not needed as much.

MAGAZINE DEADLINES

Magazines require contributors to submit their material months or weeks in advance of editing and assembling the next issue, which in itself can be several months ahead of the day the publication hits the newsstands. A monthly magazine's glossy, nationally distributed July issue may be put together in February.

This means you have to plan much farther ahead if you're submitting to a magazine than for newspapers and broadcast media. If your PR information is suitable for the summer issue of a magazine that puts out 12 or less issues per year, get your material to them by February.

Some magazines publish on a weekly or biweekly schedule and their deadlines are similar to newspapers of the same frequency.

BROADCAST MEDIA DEADLINES

Local television and radio news and features operations have tiny reporting staffs by comparison to newspapers and produce a very different news product – more visual, much less detailed and in-depth, and using far fewer words. The lead time for a TV news story is often just hours – or even "on the spot," with little or no advance preparation.

Broadcast journalism is more tolerant of submittals with short deadlines, but their airtime is short and precious for any single topic. This is particularly true for TV. Your public relations information must have high news value to land the attention of a television news director.

Radio news and features are much cheaper to produce than television news stories and, consequently, are a surer bet to gain some coverage. Local AM/FM stations are full of talk shows that focus on area newsmakers and issues of community interest and are always a likely home for public relations-based topics.

CHAPTER 7
STAFF ANNOUNCEMENTS

WHAT ARE STAFF ANNOUNCEMENTS?

Staff announcements are a special kind of news release. They present information about a person in your organization and are a staple of business sections and local-interest publications.

Such sections are usually filled with news about people in advertising, public relations, real estate, finance and other types adept at self-promotion. Because publications are glutted with staff announcements from these professions, they welcome the chance to feature people in *other* occupations.

An often-unappreciated facet of putting out a staff release is the morale boost it can give to your employees, especially the release's subject, for the recognition in the community.

If accepted by a publication, staff announcements usually result in a short story about the person with their name in bold, grouped with other similar career-advancement pieces. Often a head-and-shoulders photograph, called a "mug shot," accompanies the text.

A particularly interesting person may rate a larger story and a photograph showing them in their working environment.

REASONS TO SEND A STAFF ANNOUNCEMENT

As with other types of news releases, staff announcements will be poorly received unless they have inherent news value and interest. Following are some legitimate situations that may call for a staff announcement:

- **Hiring a new manager, specialist or someone well-known**
- **Promoting an employee**
- **Creating or filling a new position**
- **Winning a professional/industry award**
- **Becoming an officeholder in an organization or service club**
- **Announcing the manager of a new branch or location, even if a lateral move**
- **Someone in your organization does something *really* interesting**
- **New partnerships or links with other operations**
- **Ongoing service to the community and volunteering**
- **Retirement of well-known or key personnel**

Resignations, leaves of absence, marriages and such usually are not suitable subjects for staff announcements. But, if such personal decisions impact the organization or are of legitimate interest to the public, they should be handled through a news release.

WRITING YOUR STAFF ANNOUNCEMENT

Although similar in most respects to news releases, staff announcements differ in that they can be written in a specific, four-part progression:

In the *first part*, also called the "lead":
 The full name of the person comes first, before anything else
 The news about this person
 Who made the announcement

In the *second part:*
 Responsibilities of the staff member in the organization

In the *third part:*
 Education
 Professional experience and employers, including military service, if relevant
 Previous position, if relevant

In the *fourth part:*
 Organizations
 Awards and achievements
 Closing quote (optional)

Keep your staff announcement to one page. If the publication wants more detail for a larger story, they will contact you.

Most personal information, such as marital status, spouse's name, children and religion are of no interest to the audience and will detract from the release. One possible exception is a small-town newspaper, where a significant chunk of the readership may know your family members and would be motivated to read a story with their names in it.

Some kinds of personal information, like professional or amateur sports achievements, charitable work or some highly unusual facet of the subject, can be included if room allows. These newsy personal details may make your release stand out from the rest and make the staff person more interesting.

RESEARCH

Always conduct a short interview with your staff announcement subject before writing anything. Prepare for the interview by obtaining their current resume and job description.

Important – Put your questions in the order of the four parts shown above. This will help you organize your interview and keep it focused and brief. It also makes it much easier to write the release, because your information is presented in a logical progression. Always have your subject review and proofread the release before it is sent.

STAFF PHOTOS

It is common and expected to include a photograph with a staff announcement. Almost always, these photos should be a small "mug shot," showing just the head and shoulders of the individual, and usually shot with the subject directly facing the camera.

If the subject has had a professional portrait recently, that studio probably can provide prints or a digital file. Scan a print, if necessary. Don't worry about submitting anything larger than a 4x6, because the mug shot will be run much smaller than that in the publication.

If a photograph of the person at work has genuine interest – like, say, an alligator wrestler or billboard painter – it would be a good idea to include a photograph of them doing it. At the other end of the spectrum, no one wants to see another photo of a guy in a tie sitting at a desk in front of a computer or on the telephone.

Group staff photographs are acceptable, but remember the wider the photo, the less likely the publication will justify providing the space for it. Also, everyone in the image should be clearly and accurately identified.

CAPTIONING STAFF PHOTOS

Because mug shots included with staff announcements usually show no action – just the person's appearance – captions usually are limited to some basis information, such as:

- The person's name, which can be a shortened or nickname version of the full name in the announcement itself. Often, just the last name is run.
- The new title or position
- The business or organization name

Examples:

>   John Jones, new sous chef at Sandy's Dinner Club.

>   or:

>   Jones

Attach mug shot prints to caption sheest the same way other small prints are secured, as shown in Chapter 10. Staple the caption sheet to the staff announcement so nothing is loose.

SAMPLE STAFF ANNOUNCEMENT

On the following page is a properly written and formatted hard copy staff announcement. Note how the basic tenets of news releases are followed, but using the four-part progression previously discussed. Note the announcement is limited to one page and is doubled-spaced. An e-mail version would be single-spaced, with two spaces between paragraphs.

Pete's Golf Cars, Inc.
NEWS RELEASE

Aug. 21, 2007

FOR IMMEDIATE RELEASE
Contact: Peter Smith 602-555-7777

Lance Jones joins Pete's Golf Cars

Lance Jones has joined Pete's Golf Cars as chief mechanic at its Tucson location. The announcement was made by Pete's owner and president, Peter Smith.

As chief mechanic, Jones will oversee all repair and maintenance work, as well as manage warranty compliance. He also will serve as pit boss for the company's racing golf cart team, the Flaming Cucarachas.

Jones, 46, brings more than 20 years experience in golf car repair to his new position. He previously was head of golf maintenance for the Rancho Santiago Golf Resort in Hamilton, Texas.

He is a graduate of the West Texas Technical Institute with an A.S. degree in mechanical engineering and served six years in the Air Force as a mechanic.

Jones was recognized in 1996 as the Southwest's top golf car mechanic when he won first place in the Las Vegas Golf Car Fix Frenzy, where contestants must diagnose and repair various problems while competing against the clock.

"The addition of Lance Jones to our organization will prove to be a valuable asset to the entire Tucson-area golfing community," Smith said.

###

WHAT ARE FACT SHEETS?

Fact sheets are brief compilations of facts and statistics intended to help reporters produce their stories faster and more accurately. They're produced ahead of time and kept on hand to distribute to the media as needed.

Fact sheets can be included with news releases or in media kits, and can make your publicity more attractive by saving a lot of time and work for reporters.

Fact sheets should be limited to a single page if possible. This usually is not a problem, because the information they contain is basic and has little or no narrative. Don't hesitate to produce a longer fact sheet, as long the information in it is concise and to the point.

Clearly label your fact sheet with the header "FACT SHEET," followed by the company or organization name and the month and year the fact sheet was written. Including the date is important, to prevent the media from using old information and to let them know to discard or ignore any older fact sheets they might have.

A fact sheet should be reviewed and updated regularly to ensure its accuracy.

Like most PR materials, it is accepted practice to e-mail fact sheets to the media. In fact, it is the preferred method, because e-mailed text can be directly imported into a news story or other media documents without laborious and error-prone retyping.

Unlike printed news release text, fact sheets do not have to be double-spaced, because the information in them is for reference only and probably won't be edited. On rare occasions, a publication will run portions of fact sheet information exactly as they were submitted.

THE THREE ESSENTIAL TYPES OF FACT SHEETS:

- **Basic general information on a business or organization**

- **Information on an event**

- **Biographical summaries**

BUSINESS OR ORGANIZATION FACT SHEETS SHOULD HAVE:

- A brief description of the operation – Typically not more than about 50 words.

- All locations and addresses.

- Contacts – Telephone numbers, Web sites, e-mail addresses.

- Descriptions of all the facilities, giving square footage, number of employees, special equipment, etc.

- Name and titles for key personnel.

- Basic financial information.

- Statistics - Number of employees, size/cost of facilities, descriptions of products and services, major customers, regulating or accrediting agencies.

- History – How long in operation.

- Professional affiliations, awards, sponsorships.

EVENT FACT SHEETS SHOULD HAVE:

- A brief description of the event. Typically not more than about 50 words.

- Dates, times, locations.

- Purpose.

- Sponsors or promoters identified.

- History of the event – When it began, annual attendance figures, etc.

- Contacts – Telephone numbers, Web sites, e-mail addresses.

BIOGRAPHICAL SUMMARY FACT SHEETS SHOULD HAVE:

- Up-to-date, thumbnail biographies, called "current biographical summaries," of key personnel the media may need to know about.

Biographical summaries can be a single page or several – the number of pages is not directly related to the size of an organization.

For example, a large manufacturer's fact sheet may include biographical summaries of just the president and founder, along with a few top executives, while a small theater company's fact sheet could have a thumbnail bio for every member. Bios are a good opportunity to showcase information about staff.

SAMPLE FACT SHEETS

On the following pages are examples of the three types of fact sheets: General, event and biographical.

They are in a monospaced 10-point Courier nonproportional font with one-inch margins – typical for printed public relations materials. Proportional fonts like Arial or Swiss could be used if sent to the media via e-mail.

Note that double-spacing text is not required, even for hard-copy fact sheets. This is because the fact is a reference source, not a news release. The facts it presents would help produce an accurate news story, but usually would not be copied and pasted into it.

Most of the other rules of formatting a news release apply, but contact information like telephone numbers nearly always are contained in the fact sheet body of information. If you have room at the top of the page, it's still not a bad idea to clearly show contact information.

An e-mailed fact sheet should not be longer than a printed version. Keep it to the equivalent of a single printed page – about 250 words – if possible.

FACT SHEET
Pete's Golf Cars Inc.

November 2007

Description

Golf car sales and service in the Tucson and Green Valley areas. New sales include Turf Rover, Yazuguchi, Excel-CR and Scoot. Special services include upholstery, custom trailers and high-performance parts and installation.

Locations and contact numbers

Main office: 8888 E. Main St., Tucson, Ariz. 85790   602-555-7777
Green Valley: 2222 S. Busy Drive, Green Valley, Ariz. 85899   602-555-7771
Web site — www.petesgolfcars.com

Hours of operation

Monday — Saturday, 8 a.m. to 7 p.m., Sunday, 10 a.m. to 5 p.m.
Main office closed weekends. Service and parts open Monday-Sunday.

Company Principals

Owner:	Peter M. Smith
Sales Manager:	Joyce C. Hunnicutt
Service Manager:	Walter P. Scott
Chief Mechanic:	Daniel C. "Goodwrench" Goodwin
Attorneys:	Dewey, Takem & Howe, Tucson
Accountants:	Frisbee & Frisbee, Tucson
Security:	Guardians Inc. and TechnoAlarm

Employment

Tucson location: 5 full-time; 3 part-time
Green Valley location: 3 full-time; 2 part-time

Financial

Incorporated in Arizona, 1978
Fiscal Year 1978-79 sales: $ 157,000
Fiscal Year 2006-07 sales: $1,820,000

Facilities

Tucson: 8888 E. Main St., in the Bozeman Business Park
                 4,000 square feet --   1,700 showroom
                                         2,300 service and parts
                 Contains overhead lift and motor-rebuilding station
                 Facility purchased from LeaseWest Inc. in 1980
Green Valley: 2222 S. Busy Drive, on the southwest corner
                 2,200 square feet --   1,000 showroom,
                                         1,200 service and parts
                 Facility owned by Pete's Golf Cars. Acquired 1988

Organizations, Awards, Sponsorships

Golf Car Dealers Association
Tucson Chamber of Commerce and Green Valley Chamber of Commerce
GCDA Golden Putter Award for Customer Satisfaction
Outstanding Business Award, Green Valley Chamber of Commerce
Sponsor/Organizer - Green Valley Golf Car Scramble
Sponsor - Green Valley Cucarachas golf car stunt team

###

<u>FACT SHEET</u>
Green Valley Golf Car Scramble

November 2007

<u>Contact:</u>
Ray Bevins, 2007 Scramble Grand Marshal
602-555-1122

<u>Web site:</u>   www.greenvalscramble.com

<u>Description</u>
      America's oldest racing event for high-performance golf cars. Modeled after the Monte Carlo Gran Prix, the race features top drivers from around the world competing on the streets of Green Valley, Ariz. at speeds exceeding 100 mph. The race is run on a 3.5-mile course for 40 laps — a total distance of 140 miles. Proceeds go toward supporting Green Valley's Southern Star Senior Center.

<u>Event dates and locations</u>

<u>Saturday, Dec. 11, 2007</u>
Opening ceremony dinner and dance, 5:30 p.m. to 11 p.m. Southern Star Senior Center, 511 E. Telegraph St., Green Valley, Ariz.

<u>Sunday, Dec. 12, 2007</u>
10 a.m. — Drivers' parade begins at starting line, 511 E. Telegraph St.

11 a.m. - Preliminary heats start

2 p.m. - Green Valley Golf Car Scramble race begins

<u>Sponsors</u>

Pete's Golf Cars Inc. 602-555-7777
Ray Bevins & Associates 602-555-8888
TriRamCo Mining 602-555-9999

<u>History</u>

The Green Valley Golf Car Scramble began as an informal gathering of high-performance golf car enthusiasts in Green Valley in the late 1980s. The first organized race, then called the "Green Valley Run," was held in 1991. The event ceased in 1995 due to liability concerns, but was resurrected in 1995 after support was obtained from several area businesses. Since then, the race has been held every year on the second weekend of December, affording part-time winter residents the opportunity to enjoy the event.

                                    ###

CURRENT BIOGRAPHICAL SUMMARIES
FACT SHEET
Pete's Golf Cars Inc.

November 2007

Locations and contact numbers
    Main office: 8888 E. Main St., Tucson, Ariz. 85790   602-555-7777
    Green Valley: 2222 S. Busy Drive, Green Valley, Ariz. 85899   602-555-7771
    Web site — www.petesgolfcars.com

Peter M. Smith, owner
Born: Oct. 11, 1946
Education: BS, business management, Univ. of Arizona, 1967

A lifelong Arizona resident, Peter Smith is a former USGA golf pro who worked at
several resort courses in the Phoenix area before moving to Green Valley in 1977.
A year later, he began Pete's Golf Cars. Smith is active in area charities. He is
married to Patricia Smith and the couple has two sons. The Smiths reside just
outside Green Valley.

Joyce C. Hunnicutt, sales manager
Born: June 3, 1970
Education: MBA, Univ. of Arizona, 1993; BA, media arts, Arizona State Univ., 1991

Joyce Hunnicutt joined the company in 1994 and became sales manager in 1996,
being promoted to that position from salesperson. She is active in area Rotary
clubs and served as the Green Valley Rotary vice-chair from 1998-99. She is an
avid golfer, tennis player and hiker.

Walter P. Scott, service manager
Born: April 22, 1958
Education: AA, general studies, Pima Community College, 1988

Walter Scott joined Pete's Golf Cars in 1990 as a salesman, and was promoted to
service manager in 1994. His commitment to customer satisfaction was recognized
in 1996 with the Golden Service Star award from the national Golf Car Dealers
Association.

Daniel C. "Goodwrench" Goodwin, chief mechanic:
Born: Jan. 16, 1979
Education: Certificate of Competence, Burman Technical Collage, 2000
        Turf Rider Master Mechanic School, 2002

Daniel "Goodwrench" Goodwin directs a crew of three mechanics at the Pete's Golf
Cars Green Valley location and a crew of two at the Tucson location. From 2004 to
2007, he competed in the industry's Golf Car Troubleshoot Showdown, where he was
awarded first place in 2006 and consistently finished in the top three each year.

Goodwin also competes on the golf car racing circuit, driving a car he personally
maintains. He is sponsored by Pete's Golf Cars.

###

WHAT IS A 'FEATURE'?

"Hard news" is the reporting of what happens in the world – crime, politics, natural disasters, wars, scandals, accidents, financial doings and the like. Features, on the other hand, are meant to be primarily entertaining and informative, in varying proportions. Features are the human-interest stories and the pieces that delve into stuff that's engaging, but not necessarily important or crucial to know.

Feature stories are everywhere in the print and broadcast media. Much of the average newspaper consists of features, and most magazines are entirely features. Radio and television news shows also do broadcast feature stories.

Features are aimed at the curious, motivated reader who does more than scan the headlines, lead paragraphs and photos, or the TV audience that sticks around after the top news stories are aired.

Consequently, features usually are put together very differently than a straightforward new stories or news releases, with their familiar "inverted pyramid" structure of important facts or quotes at the top and less-critical stuff at the bottom.

Features are flexible in structure and use information in whatever order fits the need to tell the story. Features also can eschew the summary lead of news stories and employ more-creative types of leads to generate attention and interest in them.

WHY THE MEDIA WANTS FEATURES

A media operation is a relentless treadmill of information-gathering, with the staff scrambling most of the time to produce or find interesting content to fill the space between ads on the pages or broadcast air time between commercials.

In this atmosphere of high demand and short deadlines for stories, it's not surprising that well-written, accurate and interesting features submitted by PR specialists are welcome.

Cooperative news organizations like the Associated Press make features available to their members on a wide variety of topics. News syndicates send copyright-free features, many generated by public relations departments, to publications to fill their pages.

PR-generated features that focus on local people, businesses and topics will rise to the top of an editor's basket. This is exactly the type of product that a motivated small business or organization can provide.

HOW BROADCAST MEDIA USES WRITTEN FEATURES

Print and broadcast media operations feed off each other for ideas. Think of how often you've read a story in the morning newspaper and then see the exact same thing on the evening television news, or vice versa.

A written feature you submit to the print media also is good to send to broadcast media. If radio and TV stations use your feature as a lead to do a story of their own, they'll be able to reference the feature for background information.

TYPES OF FEATURES

No doubt the various kinds of features could be broken down into thousands of types, but the following list is as useful as any. Many features combine at least two of these broad categories. For example, a profile of an automotive inventor in a magazine could combine the personality profile, hobby and technical type of feature.

The key is to be flexible and be proficient in many types of feature writing. At the same time, subjects that you like and are familiar with should become your anchor and mainstay. It's more comfortable to write about things you know and have "expert" knowledge of, whether it's rearing young horses or coping with office politics. You have many worthwhile things to say from your life experiences that others will be interested in reading about.

Personality Profile
This is a very common type of feature that can be seen in any Sunday paper supplement, celebrity magazines, business publications, hobbyist magazines and news magazines. It tries to present the essential facts about a person, while at the same time delivering something new or unexpected to the reader. This type of feature is a good learning exercise for non-news public relations writing and interviewing techniques. Even the shortest personality profile should present the subject as the complex human being they surely are.

The "Something-Out-of-Nothing" Feature
This feature takes the seemingly insignificant stuff of life and presents it in enjoyable detail, with subjects like the "Give a Penny – Take a Penny" cups in stores, or "Do people who wield sledgehammers all day long develop a longer arm on one side?" The field is wide open, but the writer risks producing an insignificant feature about an insignificant topic.

Social Commentary
Drawing from society's stockpile of prejudice, injustice, criminal behavior and sundry other problems that need correcting, it is tempting to comment that this type of feature will never lack for story ideas, but it also can showcase people and programs that are helping make the world a better place. Some of the most compelling and important writing ever published were social commentary features. An open mind will produce the best feature.

No matter how close to your heart the subject is, maintain some distance and perspective. Present the situation and refrain from preaching or editorializing.

Historical

Every publication seems to have a need for the historical feature. It describes an interesting incident or situation in the past, such as the day Confederate troops entered the city or how area motorists in the 1920s and 1930s used to hang dead rattlesnakes on a tree at a certain the intersection.

At some point, usually at the beginning or the end of the piece, the historical feature should return to the present and make a solid connection with today's audience. How does the area look now? Have people's attitudes changed? Is anyone still alive who remembers the way things used to be?

Gonzo

This form of feature, popularized by the late Hunter S. Thompson's pieces in magazines like "Rolling Stone," ignores most the rules of "good" journalism and works its charm in other ways. The writer is the center of the action, and all facets of reality are viewed through their personal filter. Often, the original assignment is pushed aside by some new angle the writer finds more interesting.

Anyone who has read Thompson's accounts of the Pulitzer divorce trial in Florida or the Honolulu marathon will know just how far he can stray from his intended subject matter. Still, the reader somehow ends up learning a lot about the assigned topic, from an entertaining and gritty perspective. This is a personal viewpoint-type feature, where use of the "I" voice is acceptable.

Gonzo stresses a lot of personal involvement in the action by the writer, whether as a participant or spectator. Good sources for sample gonzo features are Thompson's "The Great Shark Hunt," "Kingdom of Fear" and "Generation of Swine" – books containing dozens of works that originally appeared in magazines and newspapers.

Are gonzo features acceptable PR submittals to the media? They seem to be on an upsurge, at least from freelance writers, and can be found in local alternative press-type publications. Because they work best in a rambling, sidetracked form, gonzo features tend to be longer than most other types of features and this may limit their appeal to editors.

"How-To"

What these features try to accomplish is self-explanatory: How to *do* something – Brush a cat properly, clean silk ties, stain and preserve redwood, etc. It relies on expert sources of information, and the success of the feature depends on the ability of the writer to understand and communicate a process, perhaps along with some personal experience and expertise.

"How-To" features are commonly found in newspaper Home sections, handyman magazines, home and gardening publications and niche magazines catering to independent types.

Consumer

Consumer features answer the questions, "What to buy" or perhaps most importantly, "How to save money." Included in this category are food, automotive, fashion, home furnishings, electronics, recreational equipment, investing, etc. Like the "How-to" features, these rely on expert information sources, hands-on experience and a great deal of good judgment on the part of the writer.

Technical or Trade

One of the richest markets for free-lance and staff PR writers are the thousands of specialty technical or trade publications published for readers in distinct groups, such as electrical component buyers, hydroponic farmers or radio astronomers. These magazines rely heavily on outside submissions because their staffs are small and usually do not have the budget to travel and research regional stories.

Unlike other types of features, technical or trade stories can use jargon of the readership and often can assume that some pretty esoteric information is common knowledge among them. It is almost impossible for a writer to produce a good article in this field without already having experience in it. The opportunities to make embarrassing mistakes in a feature about, for example, "the effects on molybdenum recovery in a copper-primary concentrator using autogenous mills in place of rod units" would be enough to scare off most prudent writers who lack at least a decade of mining engineering experience.

Business

A business feature can be almost any of the other types on this list, but the slant changes: Readers will want to know details like dollar amounts, corporate structure, position titles and responsibilities, how did success or failure come about and most of all, what is planned or predicted for the *future*.

Practically every newspaper has a business section, and business-oriented magazines are published for local audiences in every large city. Included under the business feature umbrella are staff announcements and profiles, as covered in Chapter 7.

Hobby

These are the light-hearted cousins of the technical or trade features. Most of us spend a lot of time at seemingly useless pursuits, such as chess, needlepoint, model airplanes, collecting silverware, etc. For the free-lancer, the good news is that there are literally thousands of hobby magazines to entertain devotees of doll restoration or raising koi. These magazines typically have very small staffs and depend on contributions from talented and knowledgeable free-lance writers/photographers, including PR people.

Like the technical feature, hobby articles can use esoteric jargon familiar to a circle of enthusiasts and can assume that a great deal of specialized information is already in the readers' minds. Writers active in the avocation themselves are best qualified to produce a quality piece of interest to such specialized readerships.

News Features

News features and color stories are usually keyed to news stories and are run while the news is still hot. The news feature presents the background or situation of a news event with more personal style than a straight news story.

A color story attempts to give the reader a true and lively description of *what it was like to be there* – the excitement of the crowd; the heat of the fire; the anger of the demonstrators; the prevailing mood. Color stories are often run as "sidebars" to news stories.

News features usually are the work of newspaper or magazine staffers, who have the contacts and resources to create a story quickly to accompany hard news on the same subject. Ongoing situations, such as tips on repairing damage from local floods, might present some news feature opportunities for an organization's PR specialist, but selling the idea to an editor would be a real accomplishment. Stick to a news release in this situation.

Issues Features

Closely related to news features, issues-oriented stories deal with those situations that have yet to be resolved, and most likely will be solved or worsened by human action. The issues feature tries to present facts – and some information new to most people – to give readers a new perspective on the issue.

Always put a human face on a feature. For example, a *news story* on the Central Arizona Project might focus on a construction delay caused by a break in the aqueduct and what it will cost to fix, how long to repair, etc. An *issues feature* might examine the history of such wall failures, with the viewpoints of the construction workers. Or it could detail the impact on a few homeowners living along the canal.

Another feature, dealing with restrictions on ATV use on public land, might focus on what local teenagers with "quads" do, now that a favorite stretch of sand near home is closed. Are they getting into trouble? A nice counterpoint to the frustration of the ATVers might be color commentary from grateful neighbors, happy that the noise and dust has abated. Mix in quotes from police and county officials, and you have the all the ingredients needed for a good issues-oriented feature story.

Microcosm

The microcosm paints a picture of a complete world unseen to most readers: The small world of a homebound quadriplegic, a support center for people with cerebral palsy or radical skateboarders living in a fringe society of their own making. It concentrates on the small to illustrate the large.

The microcosm puts demands on descriptive writing. Readers will be drawn to the story by detail and color, by appearances and impressions. Choose subjects that can be effectively described in a few pages or limit the scope of the feature to something manageable. For example, forget about trying to describe gang crime in all of Mexico City, and instead focus on a single street corner, where an adolescent gang rules its hundred-foot-diameter realm.

Anecdotal

The anecdotal feature is probably one of the most alluring types of writing to the beginning writer – and probably one of the least saleable. When was the last time you can remember reading a feature on "The day Uncle Harvey's dog got caught in the corn crib," or "Some funny things that happened to me when I moved to Fresno?" Anecdotal features are now the almost-exclusive realm of regular columnists. Should you avoid anecdotal features? By no means, just be aware they are a hard sell and are not often accepted by the media.

Humorous

Every feature, even the grimmest, can be leavened with a dollop of humor, but sustaining the humorous vein for an entire feature story is a real accomplishment. The key is to pick a subject that is so inherently funny or ridiculous that the humor is effortless and readily apparent.

For example, how could a competent writer miss with a feature on Pentagon spending? The parade of $1,200 toilet seats and $600 hammers is a humor writer's paradise. And there's no shortage of eccentrics, official dopiness and eyesores to keep the alert feature writer busy for a lifetime.

While writing a humorous feature on funny local street names, I found so many goofy street facts from just a few hours at a historical society's library that I had put off writing the feature until I could boil all the usable stuff down to a manageable length.

Slice-of-Time

The slice-of-time feature is like a clock or the old "Dragnet" series, with every incident described tagged with the day or time of day. For example:

```
2:30 a.m. - The two patrolmen are getting uneasy. The
black Ford still hasn't shown up for the drug deal. It
seems the dealers may have been tipped off.

2:48 a.m. - Moving slowly, the black Ford glides around
the corner and stops in front of the suspect's house.
Officer Higgins calls in for backup.
```

Of course, the slice-of-time feature usually requires that the writer be present at the action described to be authoritative and to be able to convey the immediacy of what's happening.

Travel

This is another type of feature that usually requires the writer to be present at the scene. Travel features emphasize a cosmopolitan attitude and tolerance for other cultures and societies. What most tourists seem to lack is a sense of history in appreciating the places they've been to, and travel feature writers should thoroughly background themselves in the particular place they want to write about, even if they've been there a dozen times.

Think how much richer a feature on Miami could be if the author spent an evening reading up on the history of the city to color the impressions of the place today.

Interviews

Many types of features involve interviewing in the research stage, but the interview feature consists of a brief introductory lead followed by the body of the story, drawn from the subject's answer to questions. The simplest form is the question-and-answer format, but this can be dull. Most interview features compile the questions and answers into prose paragraphs that mix background information with interesting details, such as a description of the room in which the interview takes place or the sound of construction outside.

Your interview questions wear several hats: Many should be prepared beforehand, based on thorough research of your subject. They should act as transitions, with a natural progression from the last answer to the next question. Interviewers should be flexible, ready to depart from the prepared format should a new and important line of conversation develop, and they should be disciplined and able to return to the point of the interview should the topic wander afield.

I see very few interview features in print that began as a public relations submittal. Most published interviews are the product of staff writers. It's usually more productive and cost-effective to *offer* an interview to the media than try to do the interview yourself.

FEATURE STRUCTURE

A feature can be written in the same "inverted pyramid" form used to write news stories, complete with a summary lead, but this usually is not the case. Feature stories can be developed gradually to build interest, using creative tools like suspense, shock and rich descriptions of setting and atmosphere.

Their structure is more flexible than hard news stories and they are meant to be read all the way until the end – which in itself is an important part of the story, unlike the diminished-importance aspect of the last paragraphs of an inverted pyramid story.

Still, there is a basic underlying logic to the way a feature usually is put together, with paragraphs of information or quotes linked to each other by transitions.

STRUCTURE OF A FEATURE

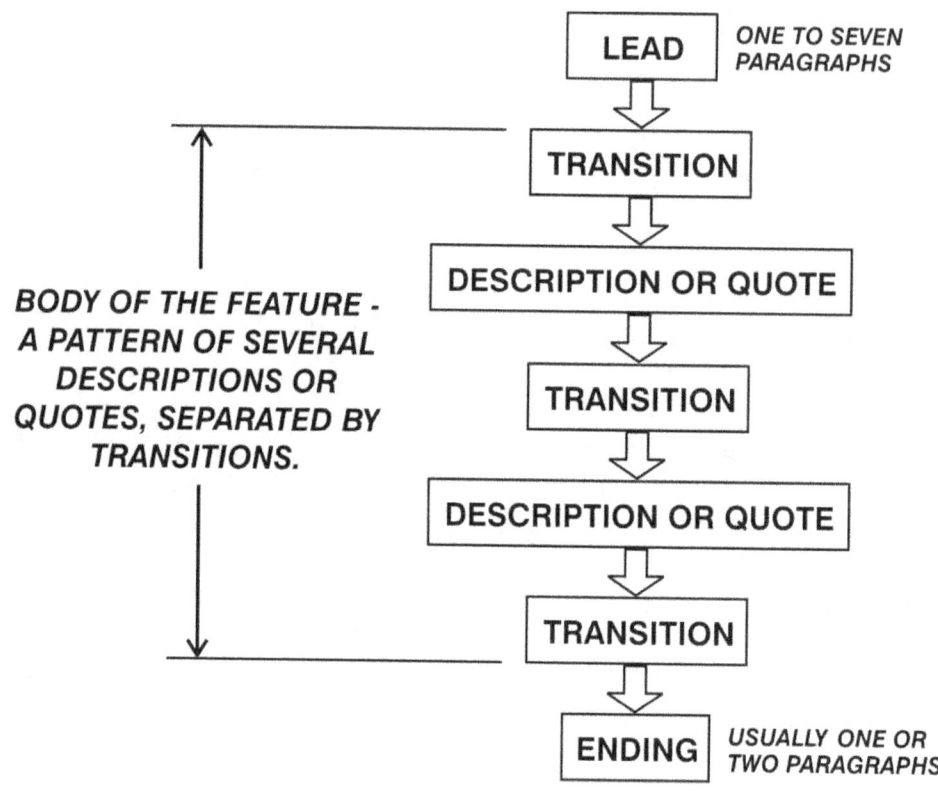

LEAD — *ONE TO SEVEN PARAGRAPHS*

TRANSITION

DESCRIPTION OR QUOTE

TRANSITION

DESCRIPTION OR QUOTE

TRANSITION

ENDING — *USUALLY ONE OR TWO PARAGRAPHS*

BODY OF THE FEATURE - A PATTERN OF SEVERAL DESCRIPTIONS OR QUOTES, SEPARATED BY TRANSITIONS.

FEATURE LEADS

Unlike lead paragraphs for news stories, feature leads do not attempt to present all important information in the first three "grafs." The purpose of a feature lead is to get the reader's attention and entice them to continue reading the story. Indeed, rather than be information-intensive, the feature lead often can accomplish its purpose by deliberately being mysterious, puzzling or contradictory.

Feature leads differ from news leads in significant ways:

- Feature leads do not need to provide the *who, where, when, what and how* of its story in the first few paragraphs. This may, in fact, detract from the mood or pace of the feature.

- Feature leads are much longer than news leads – as long as five to seven paragraphs. Because these leads are meant to appeal to readers' gut reactions, emotions and interests, it may have to be that long to set a scene, describe a character or situation or acquaint the reader with unusual circumstances. While the rules for feature leads are considerably looser than news, it usually is still a good idea to make the point as quickly as possible and get on with the story.

- As with the body of the feature, a feature lead has a much looser structure than a news lead. Sentences can be longer and paragraphs can mix description, dialogue, quotes, personal impressions, fragments of thoughts, etc. Attribution of statements or facts can be delayed and time elements can be presented later in the story.

The form of the feature lead can be chosen to fit the story. The kind of lead you choose for a feature must be determined by the story itself. Ask yourself, "What is the point of this feature? Why am I writing it? What reaction do I hope to generate in the reader?

TYPES OF FEATURE LEADS

There probably are at least as many kinds of feature leads as there are kinds of features, and any attempt to present a list should carry a caveat that it's by no means complete, but presented to give an idea of the scope of options available to the feature writer.

Summary
This type of lead is used principally on news features. Unlike most feature leads, it provides readers with the most important basic elements of the story. It also provides an overview of a situation. It summarizes the beginning, middle and end of the story, and there is no effort to generate suspense.

Quote
The quote lead must encapsulate the essence of the story. They should be short and contain attribution in the first or second paragraph. Quotes also should have very few vague words, such as "we," "they" or "many Americans." The reader will wonder who these people are, or worse, fail to identify with the writer's assumption that they will feel a certain way or know certain facts already. And just because a quote is especially bizarre or dramatic does not mean it will be an effective way to begin the story.

Direct Address
This lead addresses the reader in the second person. It is used most frequently in consumer and "how-to" articles. Unpopular for years, this lead is more in vogue today as editors seek to personalize their publications.

Nevertheless, use this lead sparingly. Unless the story screams for direct reader contact, use of words like "you," "your" or "we" can end up sounding condescending, phony or just plain dumb. Still, direct address can be a useful tool to connect with the reader at the very beginning of a feature. For example:

```
If your car is hard to start and gets poor mileage, it
may be time to change spark plugs.
```

or,

> If you have worked long enough for a private company to earn a pension, don't worry that your money will ever be taken away from you. Congress has just passed a law protecting 30 million Americans covered by such plans.

Play on Words

These leads involve puns or other humorous wordplay. This lead is either perfect or terrible, so watch out! Examples:

> Tucson television personality Michael Goodrich has been feeling under the weather for more than 20 years.

or,

> Investing in naturally harvested sea salt seemed like a sure-fire way to get rich for Jim and Marge Reed, but three years and $20,000 later, they have seen their life savings evaporate.

Question

This is another lead that should be used sparingly. The question must be very short and must sum up the story. Examples:

> What happens to an anti-war organization when the war ends?

or,

> With all the low-cost electronic calculators for sale, how did Keuffel & Esser sell more than 300,000 slide rules last year?

Staccato

This imitates the brusque and information-intensive way of speaking popularized by detective novels and movies of the 1940s and '50s. Picture Humphrey Bogart or Jack Webb speaking the lead. Again, use sparingly – only if the lead suits the mood or subject matter perfectly. Staccato leads can create suspense and often fits subjects such as prisons, police matters, drugs and the "darker side of life." For example:

> Joe's first day in his new home. Ten by ten and an arsonist for a roommate. No chance of parole for seven years.

or,

> In a rural bar near Arivaca. Nearly midnight. The regulars are having a good time. Until the Franco brothers walk in.

Contrast

This lead contrasts or compares one thing with another or several things with each other, and sometimes are called "then and now" or "short and tall" leads. They frequently are used with historical features. A contrast lead is very effective if you can get an interesting angle. Try contrasting something other than time, age or appearance. For example:

> When Harvey Lavan van Cliburn of Kilgore, Texas, left last week for the Tchaikovsky International Piano Competition in Moscow, he had three suitcases. When he returned home yesterday, he had 17. They bespoke his triumph.

or,

> Eugene W. Phillips stumbled and fell from his porch, punctured his back with a stick and slammed his head against the ground. It was just about the nicest thing that ever happened to him.
>
> Phillips had been blind for the past 16 years. The accident a week ago mysteriously restored his sight.

Shock

These leads startle readers, compelling them to read on. A major pitfall is that writers can go to extremes to create shock leads, resulting in readers forming incorrect initial impressions of the story that are distasteful and unwarranted. This first example is in *questionable* taste:

> An Edgewood, Idaho, city police officer says he would like to shoot people all day long if it would make the streets any safer.
>
> "It's easy. Take the gun, aim and shoot. Whammo! You've nailed 'em," patrolman Lance W. Dobbins said.
>
> He spends about two hours a day hidden in bushes or behind a billboard, waiting for the unsuspecting speeder to cross the sights of his radar gun.

or,

> Some personal secrets can kill you.
>
> That's why many people are making them public. The list includes persons such as Sylvester Stallone, Dolly Parton and Joe Montana.
>
> These famous faces and many average people are proud owners of Medic-Alert bracelets, warning of serious medical problems or drug allergies.

Suspense

These are designed to attract the reader's curiosity. The best suspense leads usually are short. Examples:

```
Karen Martin no longer wonders who she is.
```

or,

```
Three weeks ago, Sue Jones bought a stack of national park
guidebooks, planning a cross-country camping trip for her
husband and herself. Two days later, she bought a coffin.
```

Atmosphere

These set out to attract readers by setting up a mood. Good atmosphere leads require well-developed descriptive writing skills. The important thing to remember is that restraint is vital. *Show* readers what a place looked like or smelled like, don't *tell* them. Concentrate on the use of facts, not adjectives. For example:

```
A rainy afternoon in the forest and sugarcane country of
central Louisiana. Not much is happening in the city of
Glendora. Downtown, a third of the businesses are boarded
up. Outside McQueen's, a dingy, tin-roofed cafe surrounded
by empty buildings, some jobless men are drinking beer.

A rusty pickup truck heaped with sacks of sweet potatoes
chugs past, and a small boy riding in the back grins,
holding up a couple of dollar bills - proof that some
money still can be made in these parts.

The loiterers snort. "Selling sweet potatoes. That's about
the only kind of job in Glendora," says one.

As goes Glendora, so, more or less, goes this part of
Louisiana. Basic industries are languishing; hope is a
scarce commodity.
```

Setting

This lead describes the *place* where the action occurs. It is closely related to the atmosphere lead, but doesn't necessarily try to set a mood. Setting leads are particularly appropriate when the place where the action occurs is itself central to the impact of the story, for example:

```
The cellblock is filled with trash, excrement and spoiled
food, all of it soaked with water collected in puddles.
The air reeks of tear gas and smoke. A pile of bedding is
on fire and all the windows are closed. Prisoners scream
and clang the bars.
```

This may sound like a description of the Pontiac State
Prison at the height of the riot there last July, when
three guards were killed and three others seriously
injured. And it may have been like that then.

But this was Pontiac State Prison on Oct. 11, almost three
months after the riot. It was the scene as I entered
Cellblock A to begin my first day as a prison guard.

Physical Description

This involves describing a person's appearance in the lead. It should be done only when
the person is a major character or the focus of the feature and when the person's
appearance is an important aspect of the piece. Additionally, the person's appearance must
be interesting in itself. Example:

The Man Who Stands in Two Places is getting old.

Seventy-four years are printed on his face. Wrinkles have
eroded into small canyons cutting across his forehead and
down each side of his nose. His left eyelid flutters over
an empty socket: The eye was removed two years ago, when
it went blind and began giving him pain.

It no longer hurts, but his good eye waters constantly and
he dabs it with a paper napkin. His hair is twisted in a
braid more gray than black. At his neck is a bead totem.

Anecdotal

These leads have become extremely popular in the last decade. Like direct address leads,
they reflect an effort by editors to personalize the stories in their newspapers. Anecdote
leads come in three basic flavors: "Once Upon a Time," "Narrative" and "What If."

The **once upon a time** lead describes an incident in the past. Many historical features
begin this way. For example:

The 14-year-old girl was smarting from the latest beating
by the matron who ruled her floor of the decrepit
orphanage when she approached the high wall in the dark.
Once over, she would be free, but facing an uncertain
future in the rough-and-tumble world of frontier Arizona.

Climbing the rough adobe blocks, she reached the top and
gazed into the inky desert darkness. Somewhere in the
distance, a coyote sang. It was then Mary Smith made her
fateful decision and dropped back into the yard of the
hated orphanage.

```
She determined to stay and fight for better conditions,
never dreaming one day she would be in charge of the very
institution she tried to flee.
```

The **narrative** anecdotal lead follows one of the main characters as they do whatever action the feature is focused upon. The action described in the past must be central to the point of the story and usually is written in the present tense. Example:

```
Every night after making her rounds, the white-haired
woman shuffles in her slippers to the living room, where
she opens a pull-out couch into a bed.

She lies on a thin, sagging mattress and closes her eyes,
sleeping lightly, so that she will hear if anyone awakens
during the night.

This has been Doris Hatfield's routine since 1981, when
she officially turned her rural Orlando home, set back
from a dirt road off Holden Avenue, into an institution
for the mentally ill.
```

The third type of anecdote lead is the "**what if**" lead, describing a hypothetical incident. It is usually for stories that concern a future event or a new trend that is expected to have significant impact in the coming months or years.

Many "what if" leads are also *direct address* leads. Writers combine the two techniques to draw readers into the story immediately and to make the story more relevant to their lives, for example:

```
Your lawn is mowed, the laundry is washed and dried, and
the dog's been walked. All before you leave for work at 7
a.m. All that remains is to make sure the household robots
that actually did all this work are back at their
recharging stations.

Welcome to your life 20 years from now, if some consumer
futurists can be believed.
```

Microcosm
This is a grab-bag combination of other leads. It can involve narration, atmosphere, setting, dialogue, and most often is part of a microcosm-type feature. These leads work hard to point out as soon as possible that the person or things featured in the first few sentences is representative of a group.

These leads and bodies of such features concentrate on showing readers the impact of some larger situation, trend or event by going into detail about how it has affected one individual, family or group.

Microcosm leads work well to introduce readers to a little-known subculture or part of the world, like a street gang or the closed-in world of a paraplegic. Example:

```
Tim likes to read travel magazines, but he cannot even
leave his own house.
```

Analogy

Using an analogy – writing about a baseball team in terms of a family; pets of the elderly as children; a birdwatching club's outing as a safari – is a good way to introduce humor and life into what might otherwise be a somewhat dry topic.

An analogy also sets up the feature for an analogy *ending* if the feature isn't so long that the reader has forgotten the clever comparison by the time they reach the ending. It works best on shorter features.

And remember, leave the whole analogy concept after the lead and don't pick it up again until the ending. It is easy to see how overdrawn and tiring a sustained analogy could become in a feature-length story.

```
The guide motions his clients forward, advising in hushed
tones to be as quiet as possible. The small group of men
and women in safari hats inch forward through the thick
undergrowth. The air of tense anticipation is almost
palpable.

At last, the quarry is in sight. The long, bumpy drive
through difficult backcountry is about to pay off.
Expensive optics slide silently from padded cases. The
woman closest to the target takes aim.

Her binoculars reveal every exquisite detail of the
skittish downy woodpecker.
```

TRANSITIONS

Transitions are words, phrases, sentences – but most often paragraphs – that link separate parts of a feature story. They serve as a natural bridge to link shifts in time, place, speaker, emphasis, etc. They sew the story into a seamless whole.

From the transition examples that follow, it's easy to see how they can lead from one paragraph to another. A paragraph about a successful community charity could be followed by a transition linking it to a new paragraph about a charity operation in financial trouble.

Transitions can be statements of fact, introducing other voices, places, times:

> Williams' views are considered revolutionary by many researchers.

> Placita del Sol is only one of more than a dozen such operations in the city.

> The intersection of Broadway and Wilmot Road is a much different place than it was 20 years ago.

Or quotes:

> "So we asked ourselves, who could build such a thing?"

> "I was fed up. I couldn't take any more. That's when I signed up."

Or a reflection of the lead, linking to it by repetition:

> Sometimes things that come down the sewer are the stuff dreams are made of.

> Getting high on risk-taking can involve more than your money or career: Some people enjoy putting their very life on the line.

Or questions:

> Now that they had the money, what were they going to do with it?

> How many votes could the candidate expect?

Or statements of contrast:

> On the city's south side, another halfway house is not so fortunate.

> For those with less than $10,000 to spend on a wedding dress, lots of options are available.

Or statements of similarity:

```
Mainstream clergy aren't the only ones worried about
declining attendance at church services.

Despite a bonanza of perks and security, the Japanese
autoworker shares many concerns with his American
counterpart.
```

Using the paragraph-transition-paragraph structure, a feature story can quickly be created in an easy-to-write, easy-to-read flow of ideas. Features of any length, from 250-word "featurettes" to 10,000-word magazine centerpieces, are put together this way.

FEATURE WRITING IS BEST LEARNED BY DOING

Features are much of what is in a newspaper and most of what fills nearly every magazine on the stands. People read or watch features every day without thinking what makes them different than hard news.

Recognize the elements that go into writing a feature as you read one and see how its author crafted an interesting piece that looks almost free-form, but in fact adheres to a recognizable pattern of effective word flow.

The next step in becoming a proficient feature writer for your public relations program would be to attend a class on feature writing, one that stresses producing features for publication. Most writing classes veer far afield of the type of story that newspapers or magazines want to see. Try to find a class that identifies itself as a journalism or media studies course, not English or "creative writing."

If a class is not available in your area, purchase one of the feature-writing texts or guides listed in Chapter 17 – Reference Resources. These books can help, but nothing is better than the discipline of sitting in a class every week and having to actually write features on deadlines, often on subjects not of your own choosing.

Unlike a lot of newswriting – and news *reading* – features should be fun to write and read. They're meant to both inform and entertain, and will prove to be a valuable part of your public relations efforts. Well-written, interesting and fact-filled features can find acceptance in the media markets you need to reach.

PUBLIC RELATIONS PHOTOGRAPHY

Photographs often accompany news releases, staff announcements and media kits. They help "sell" the information to the media by enhancing the text and providing explanation or detail. Often, a publication will run only the captioned photo that was submitted with a news release. Including a photograph may catch an editor's eye in a way plain text cannot.

Serviceable photographs also will make the release more attractive by possibly eliminating the need for the publication to send a photographer of their own.

Public relations photography can be considered a branch of photojournalism: the techniques and markets are similar. It is sometimes referred to as **"editorial photography,"** and professional photographers frequently advertise their expertise in editorial work. Public relations photos are quite different from art photography or portrait studio work, with an emphasis on clarity and content, not style or artistic impact. Like news photos, the center of attention usually should be people, particularly faces.

WHY DO THE PHOTOGRAPHY YOURSELF?

- Editorial photography is very straightforward and good results can be obtained by anyone who masters the basics of photography. Taking the time to learn your camera will be a profitable investment.

- Professional photographers charge $60 an hour and up for editorial work. With a little effort, you can limit the expense involved to your time and the cost of a capable point-and-shoot digital camera. Many pro photographers will insist on keeping the images files or negatives of the work they do for you, forcing you to use them every time you need additional copies. And a pro photographer who's good with portraits, weddings, fine art, architecture or landscapes isn't necessarily adept at editorial work.

- With basic photographic skills and equipment available in-house, a small business or organization can take advantage of spur-of-the-moment opportunities and "grab shots." And if a photo session doesn't yield the results you want, just get the camera and redo it, learning from your mistakes.

- Finally, doing it yourself means being able to document things that happen over several days, months or years, such as building a new facility or getting "before and after" photos. Keeping an outside photographer around for days or repeatedly calling them back would be very expensive.

IT'S A DIGITAL WORLD

Not so long ago, public relations photography was all about choosing the right 35mm camera, lens, flash and film – and dealing with developers for slides or prints from negatives. Captions had to be typed and attached to the prints or slides in the hope that the images and the words that correctly described them would not get separated on the way to the media.

No longer. Along with submitting material via the Internet, no aspect of public relations has changed so profoundly as photography since the 1990s. Digital photography and all its related areas – image editing, file storage and sending via e-mail – now make PR photography easy, fast and affordable.

Even if you're stuck with a lot of "legacy" images in the form of prints, slides and negatives, it's a snap, using inexpensive scanners, to convert these into usable digital formats that never will get dusty, torn or water-damaged.

If you're determined to stick with film-based photography for your public relations work, the last section of this chapter deals with accepted, but low-tech, protocols for submitting prints and slides to your media recipients, along with printed captions.

DIGITAL PHOTOGRAPHY EQUIPMENT

The cost of digital cameras, scanners, associated peripherals and software continues to drop, while their capabilities, features and ease-of-use climb. At this point, there's really no good reason to consider film-based photography for public relations work.

At a minimum, you will need:

- **A digital still camera.**
- **A computer with an Internet connection.**
- **Backup devices – An optical drive to burn DVDs and an external hard drive.**
- **A flatbed or film scanner (optional).**
- **An image-editing program.**

DIGITAL STILL CAMERAS

"Digicams" come in two basic types:

- **Compact "Point-and-Shoot" cameras** with nonremovable lenses, small built-in flash units, largely automatic operation and, usually, an LCD color screen for previewing and reviewing images. They have become so inexpensive that a model ready for any kind of PR task can be had for around $100. Stick to well-known manufacturers with names you recognize, like Canon – my favorite – or Nikon. Point-and-shoots that use AA batteries are a little larger than tiny models that use thin, proprietary rechargeable batteries, but they're cheaper, easier to maintain and have larger, easier-to-use controls.

- **DSLRs – "Digital Single-Lens Reflex" cameras** that look like the familiar 35mm SLRs of old. These cameras fit a large selection of wide-angle to telephoto interchangeable lenses, specialty lenses and filters, and are packed with features and options. They will operate powerful flash units via a "hot shoe" or remote trigger and generally have high resolution and low-light capability. DSLRs cost much more than a typical point-and-shoot camera, but the extra expense may allow for better results, especially if your PR photo jobs require special lenses, faster shutter speeds or enhanced quality in dim conditions.

Understand the "megapixels" of your camera and their significance. Digital images are made up of tiny little dots of color called pixels. A million pixels equal a megapixel. The more megapixels your camera can achieve, the higher resolution will result.

Whichever camera you choose for your PR image-taker, keep in mind the requirements of the media to which you're submitting. Newspaper photos are not high-quality in terms of resolution, and images you send to papers that are at least three megapixels will be fine. Glossy magazines want better quality and probably will reject your photos if they are not at least eight megapixels – 10 and up would be preferable – and sharply focused. This would make a DSLR almost a necessity if you plan to submit to magazines.

If you choose to work with a more-expensive DSLR, remember you're also buying into a "system" of compatible lenses, flashes, memory cards and batteries. Make sure you're happy with your camera and its system before you end up with a bag full of accessories for something you're not sure you will be keeping for years..

Don't skimp on memory for your digital camera. Invest in at least a 2GB card for day-to-day operation, with another as a backup. Get a rugged padded camera case, with room for the memory cards, a spare set of fresh batteries and a small notepad and pencil.

Forget about using the camera on your cellular phone for PR work. Unless you're at the very high end of cell phone models, such cameras lack the resolution and lens quality to produce acceptable results. Images from most cell phone cameras are the modern equivalent of the "focus-free" Brownie film cameras of yesteryear.

COMPUTERS

It would be hard to find a new desktop or laptop computer on the market today that can't handle digital image editing. Make sure your machine has high-speed USB ports, used by most digicams to transfer images to the computer, and 1TB or larger hard drive.

To keep your computer from "choking" on images with big file sizes, you should have at least 4 to 6GB of RAM system memory. The memory needs of PC operating systems mean anything less than 4GB of RAM will not leave enough for image editing files. A fast processor also will speed up your photo work, but it still will be hobbled without sufficient RAM available.

Always protect your computer with a battery backup/surge-protection unit that can give you at least 15 minutes operation during a power failure to shut down and save your work.

INTERNET CONNECTION

Unless they're reduced and compressed, digital photo files are large – around 2MB to 12MB for JPEG images that are 5 to 16 megapixels in resolution. These file sizes won't be a problem for the people to whom you *send* PR photos: Any newspaper, magazine or broadcast media operation you deal with will almost certainly have a high-speed connection of some kind and will be able to download your images in seconds.

If you have a high-speed connection, then you can e-mail large image files with no problem. If you access the Internet via a slow "dial-up" connection using a modem, you may want to reduce your images in size and/or compress them to make e-mailing more practical. To do this, you will need an image-editing program – see this chapter's "Software" section, or let your e-mail program downsize them for you – at the risk of becoming unusable.

BACKUP OPTIONS

Almost as important as your camera and computer are the devices you need to store and protect your images. Do not rely on your computer's hard drive – it is a delicate mechanical device that will eventually fail or have its files corrupted by a virus or electrical problem.

Copy your image files "out of the box" to an external hard drive or recordable DVDs or CDs. This will protect them from whatever goes haywire in the computer itself. For that reason, keep your external hard drive turned off and disconnected from the computer and electrical outlet whenever you're not using it. The fewer hours it operates, the less likely it is to fail.

The external hard drive is the backup device of choice. Although it is still subject to mechanical failure, it runs a tiny fraction of the hours your computer's hard drive does, and likely will last virtually forever, as long as you take care of it. Make it your good habit to back up your files at least weekly to the external hard drive and whenever you've just finished a major piece of work.

Recordable Blu-ray BD-Rs, DVDs and CDs should be your next layer of file protection. Regularly back up your images to these optical discs and store them in a spot away from the computer, like a garage or safe-deposit box that's away from your office. If there's a fire or some other disaster, your data and images will be safe. Exercising these backup options, your valuable image files will be safely stored in at least three places at once: Your computer; your external hard drive; and DVDs/CDs stored away from the first two. It's unlikely you'll be crying over lost words or pictures.

There's another easy way you can take to secure your data and images, by configuring your programs to send periodic automatic backups to a flash memory "key drive" kept plugged in a USB port. For programs that don't feature automatic backups, try to save your work at least hourly to the key drive. Now everything is saved in *four* places. As the key drive fills, delete the older files on it that by now have been redundantly saved to both the external hard drive and a DVD. Finally, online remote data-storage facilities offer yet another viable option to safeguard your files and get them away from your dangerously fallible hard drive.

SCANNERS

Feature-rich *flatbed scanners* with high resolution and the ability to scan film negatives and slides can be had for about the same cost as a good point-and-shoot digital camera. If you have a lot of prints, negatives or slides that could be put to good use in your PR work, then do not hesitate to invest in a scanner. Even low-cost basic models will do a good job scanning color and black-and-white prints. Spend a little more for a scanner and it will include film and slide adapters, and a better suite of software – including an image-editing program with more tools and features than you're likely to need.

For best results with film negatives or slides, use a *film scanner* that is made specifically for those types of images. You won't be able to scan prints or documents with it, like a flat-bed unit can, but the results will be far superior.

IMAGE-EDITING PROGRAMS

There's nothing inherently wrong with sending unedited digital images with your public relations submittals, but photos that have been competently cropped, sized, sharpened and improved in other ways will make your photo submittals much more attractive and usable.

Well-edited images also save a lot of work for the media. Unlike magazines, newspapers aren't very picky when it comes to things like fine resolution and striking layout – they're mostly content to receive sharp, well-exposed photographs that convey something of interest to the readers. It pays to go the extra mile and supply images to the print media that are easy to place on the page and don't need a lot of tweaking to be usable,.

Popular programs such as Adobe Photoshop, Photoshop Elements and their competitors at the mid-to-high range of image-editing software have more than enough capability to handle your public relations needs. Maybe too much. Check out less expensive programs to see if they have the basic tools you need. Some free software also lets you do the job.

Most image-editing software comes with a host of powerful tools and artsy features, but resist the temptation to manipulate your digital photographs beyond cropping, resizing, contrast changes and other modest revisions. Remember, it's still a news photo you're dealing with, and whopping changes such as removing unwanted people from a group or fixing facial wrinkles, while fun, are dishonest – and sometimes illegal – practices for editorial photo work.

IMAGE FILE FORMATS

For most PR work, stick with the JPEG format, which nearly every digital camera uses as its default file type. JPEG images have reasonably small file sizes, very good quality and are easy to compress. The principal JPEG drawback is that it's a "lossy" file format, meaning it loses image quality as it's edited and resaved over time. This deterioration takes many, many saves to detect, and even then is hardly noticeable.

One way to avoid problems with lossy JPEGs over the long haul is to save the images you really want to keep absolutely pristine in a "nonlossy" file format, such as TIFF. If you're a stickler for utmost image quality, then shoot and save in RAW format .

Either way, you should still do your image editing on JPEGs and make it your standard operating procedure to submit JPEGs to newspapers. Some magazines, particularly those with high-quality paper and fine-screen printing, may want a particular file format. Check with their photo editor to find out what they require.

EDITING IMAGES FOR PR SUBMITTALS

The foremost thing to remember when you're editing a photograph for public relations purposes is that it's still a news photo and your options for manipulating it are very limited, subject to journalistic ethics and practices. The image should remain a true record of what the camera saw.

What this means is that you should limit your image editing to cropping, resizing, adjusting brightness and contrast, sharpening and filtering out "noise." Try to keep your changes few and modest. When you're finished with these manipulations, then go ahead and compress the image file if needed.

Cropping probably is the easiest and most useful way to improve an image. Because most digital cameras produce images that conform to a 4x3 rectangle – for example, 3,264 x 2,448 pixels in an 8 MB image – you will often find it possible to crop out extra sky or foreground that contribute nothing to the photo, but were unavoidable because of the image's 4x3 proportions.

Cropping is useful to lop-off unattractive or distracting photo elements near the edges of an image, such as a billboard or a scowling pedestrian passing by. Don't crop to change the essential truthfulness of a photo.

Resizing primarily is done to reduce file size. This is not an important consideration if both sender and recipient have high-speed Internet connections. Resizing also can help if the photo is likely to be run very small, such as a tiny portrait "mug shot" for the business briefs section of a newspaper.

The rule of thumb is: Newspapers run most PR-based photos fairly small – smaller than a 4x6 print – and their printing process is fairly coarse and low quality. They don't need big files. Magazines, on the other hand, typically have fine-screen printing, glossy paper and often run photos quite large. They need higher-resolution images.

Brightness and contrast adjustments are easy and often necessary to make an image usable. Newspapers prefer bright, contrasty images: They just reproduce better on off-white newsprint paper with the thin, coarse printing process most newspapers use. Newspapers can adjust your images to suit their needs, but doing the work for them increases the likelihood your photo submittal will be used.

Magazines can handle subtler tones and likely will have the staff and time to adjust your images to their liking.

Sharpening digital images is almost never needed, but can help in some cases. If your photograph has text in it, such as a banner, giant presentation check or architectural signage, it is important that the letters be as sharp and defined as possible. Remember your photo probably will be run small on the page and text-type details may need sharpening to be readable. Watch out for edge artifacts in areas of extreme light/dark transitions – This is a sign of over-sharpening.

"Noise" in a digital image is the equivalent of grain in a film-based photograph, usually due to taking the photo in dim conditions at light-sensitive, high-ISO settings. Noise shows up as a splotchy, grainy texture and is particularly noticeable in skin tones and large areas of constant tone, such as skies or interior walls.

Any competent image-editing software will allow you to reduce noise, but at the cost of some sharpness. Conversely, sharpening can increase the appearance of noise, so avoid the temptation to sharpen an already-noisy image. For newspaper placement, with its relatively crude quality, noise typically is not an important drawback.

COMPRESSION AND IMAGE FILE SIZE

Many factors determine the file size of your digital images: File format, resolution, amount of compression applied, even the number of colors in the image. For any given file format, the larger the image in megapixels, the bigger the file size.

Some image file formats, such as TIFF, create much larger file sizes than JPEGs for otherwise identical digital images. If your image is at least 5 megapixels, it will be fine for all newspaper placement and some magazines. Ten megapixels and larger is preferable for submitting to glossy magazines.

Compressing an image file can dramatically reduce its size to a fraction of the original – at the cost of some detail and overall quality – and make it much easier to submit via e-mail.

There are three common reasons to consider compressing image files:

- If you or your recipient have a slow Internet connection. A compressed file will avoid clogging-up someone's computer while your big image file comes in.

- If you are submitting more than a handful of images, even to a fast-Internet destination, think about a small amount of compression – 10 to 30 percent.

- Consider the destination of your image submittal. If it's a newspaper, overall image quality is not a big factor in the acceptability of the image: News value, content and potential reader interest *are*.

EDITORIAL PHOTO BASICS

"**Set your camera at f/8 and be there,**" is an axiom in photojournalism. It means it's more important to *get the picture* than to make sure it's perfect. Secondary, but still important, are clarity (focus, exposure) and content (subject matter, inherent image information). Use news photographers as your role models for PR work.

First and foremost, **learn your camera well and know its limitations**. Even low-end digital cameras have a ton of useful features and surprising capabilities. However, most point-and-shoots have two Achilles heels – relatively slow lenses and weak flash – that can limit their ability to produce an acceptable shot in some situations. DSLRs will be much more capable in nearly every situation, and more expensive.

Have your camera ready to go at all times. Keep the batteries charged and keep spare memory cards with the camera. A padded camera bag is vital to not only protect the camera, but to keep all your photo essentials in one place. Carry a small notebook and a digital voice recorder in your camera bag, too, for saving information about names, places and other facts that will go into the caption.

Beware of backlighting, possibly the most common cause of bad photographs. In a backlit scene, the subject is in front of a light source or bright background. Common examples are sunsets, white office walls or outdoor daylight backgrounds where the subject is in shade, such as a ramada. Because backlighting and other unfavorable light situations are everywhere and often unavoidable, it is generally a good idea to try to cancel it out with "fill" flash or full flash.

When using flash indoors, take pains to **avoid flash "monster shadows"** behind a subject when they are too close to a wall. Try to get the subject away from flat surfaces behind them and into more open areas. The darker it is in the room, the more intense the flash shadow will be. Brighten the room as much as possible by turning on lamps and opening the curtains. If you're using a DSLR with a separate powerful flash unit, employ the tilt/swivel head to bounce the flash light off the ceiling or an adjacent wall. Diffuse the flash if possible.

Use indoor flash sparingly. Instead, use higher ISO settings to get good indoor exposures without flash, and deal with any resulting noise later, when you edit the image.

Direct sunlight casts harsh shadows that are too dark and too deep, particularly at midday. Overcome it with fill or full flash. For most outdoor PR photo work, a bright overcast day provides the best light.

If your flash is close or in-line with your lens – typical for built-in flashes on point-and-shoot cameras and DSLRs – faces will show "**red-eye**" in color photos. This results from the flash firing too fast for the iris to react: It remains open during the exposure and the red interior of the eye is showing. Some cameras have red-eye reduction features. If not, bouncing the flash will help.

Red eye is much less noticeable if your image is reproduced in black-and-white, but in this case it will produce a spooky-looking giant dark pupil. Red eye is easily corrected with an image editor. Most image-editing programs can automatically detect and repair red eye.

Filters generally are not needed. A "sky" filter on your lens serves mainly to protect it from dirt. Polarizers help intensify color, and make a big improvement in sky and water subjects. Avoid color, gradient and special effects filters when you're doing editorial photography, as these devices would result in falsification of the image.

Know the common lens distortions and how to minimize them. They generally are a function of the focal length of the lens at the time of the shot: "Barrel" distortion comes from wide-angle focal lengths and makes things look curved and fatter in the middle. "Pincushion" occurs at long focal lengths and pinches the scene in the middle.

Most point-and-shoot cameras have a fixed lens that can be zoomed from mild wide angle to a modest telephoto. Only practice and familiarity with your PR camera will let you master lens distortions with confidence.

Leave your tripod at home. Most editorial photography, like news photography, depends on a mobile point-of-view. Tripods are generally useful only for architectural, landscape and telephoto shots. If you need extra stability on the run, try a monopod.

"Learn to turn": Use "portrait" format (image taller than it is wide) for pictures of one person or vertical subjects. Use "landscape" format (image wide, the default orientation for most cameras) for pictures of groups, buildings, signage – and landscapes.

Avoid the boring PR photo cliches: The person on the phone, the person at the computer keyboard, the two guys shaking hands, the smiling, static, standing group. *Real* people doing *real* things, instead of posing, results in better, more believable and realistic pictures.

Keep faces foremost. Most photographs, including public relations images, are much more interesting and relevant if people are in them and are large enough to be recognized.

How high you hold your camera creates an impression. People photographed from a low angle makes them look taller, intelligent and powerful – or, if an *unsympathetic* personality, menacing and overbearing. Photos looking down at a subject from above makes them seem helpless, weak and insignificant – or, if a *sympathetic* character, mild, harmless and worthy of assistance. Straight-on, eye-level portraits create an impression of straightforwardness, trust and empathy.

Avoid complex backgrounds like library shelves and florals. At best, they distract attention from your subject. At worst, they can make your subject look ridiculous. We've all seen photos where a tree or bush in the background magically becomes a set of antlers or a freaky haircut on the person standing in front of them.

For photos of one person accompanying a staff announcement or business feature, **use a "mug shot"** – the subject's head and shoulders should completely fill the frame. Full-body-length photos, from the feet to the top of the head, are unneeded and usually unflattering.

Do "the turn" and have your subject's torso turned slightly away from fully facing the camera, while still looking directly at the lens. This avoids the mug shot looking like an actual *police* mug shot, with the person flatly facing the camera.

Consider the dominant light source in a scene. Daylight has few problems, but fluorescent lights can lend a greenish cast to an image, and incandescent lights will turn it yellow. Most digital cameras have white balance settings that will compensate for various lighting sources, and image editors can correct light-source color casts by adding various amounts of the appropriate colors. Adding blue, for example, will correct a yellowish tone.

CAPTIONS

If your public relations submittal includes photographs, every one should be captioned following legal standards and journalistic conventions. Chapter 4 – Writing a News Release includes a section on writing captions.

LEGAL CONSIDERATIONS IN PR PHOTOGRAPHY

Most photographs in publications are captioned, and those captions are subject to the same libel laws that govern all published written work, along with the usual journalistic standards for accuracy and completeness. For more detail on the laws that govern journalism, see Chapter 15 – Legal Considerations.

Photographs also are subject to legal problems based on the concept of invasion of privacy. Innocent and proper photos can be fouled up by their placement in a publication, the nature of their use – in advertising, for example – and by being linked to the wrong caption.

Photographs can get you into trouble if they are:

- Incorrectly identifying the people in the caption.

- Used without permission – This pertains mainly to advertising.

- Published with the intent to defame or ridicule.

- Placed to associate the picture with an unrelated story.

- Offensive to accepted moral standards.

- Obtained by an invasion of privacy.

- In violation of the elements of libel.

Photographs also can lie: Optical illusions are common. For example, white objects appear larger than dark ones; horizontal stripes make things look wider; and deep depth-of-field can create relationships between distant objects that aren't true. And manipulation of digital photos by editing software can create changes to the original images that nearly are impossible to detect.

Before you submit a photograph to the media, look it over carefully – and ask a few other people to look it over, too. The way a photo shows a scene must be carefully evaluated. Are there any elements in the image that could be mistaken for something offensive or ridiculous? Is there some little detail that could ruin the good impression of the photo or be grounds for legal action?

Photographs can usually stand on their own as accurate renderings of reality. However, optical illusions and other problems can occur inadvertently, unless careful attention is paid to an image by its creator.

PHOTOGRAPHY RELEASES

The majority of legal cases involving published photographs come under the concept of right of privacy. Generally, if the photograph is to be used for profit or "purposes of trade," which is to say advertising or public relations; as a work of art that will be widely reproduced, such as a book illustration; or in conjunction with a work of fiction, it must be protected by *obtaining consent* from the subject.

Using a photography release to get consent from people in your photographs – even employees or family members – will help you avoid legal problems and allow use of the image for other purposes, such as advertising.

Copy the generic photography release form on the following page – and use it. Release forms and other written consent documents are contracts and must be signed by all parties to the agreement.

Don't worry too much about releases for photos depicting large groups. Persons who attend events open to the public may have their photograph taken as part of the audience, even though they may not desire that this be done.

Watch out, though, if one person in such a situation is prominent and stands out from the group. This person could legitimately claim their likeness is being used without permission for public relations or advertising and could file suit.

PHOTOGRAPHY RELEASE

In consideration of my engagement as a model, and for other good and valuable considerations herein acknowledged as received, I hereby grant to _____ ("Photographer"), his/her heirs, legal representatives and assigns, those for whom Photographer is acting, and those acting with his/her authority and permission, the irrevocable and unrestricted right and permission to copyright, in his/her own name or otherwise, and use, reuse, publish and republish photographic portraits or pictures of me or in which I may be included, in whole or in part, or composite or distorted in character or form, without restriction as to changes or alterations, in conjunction with my own or a fictitious name, or reproductions thereof in color or otherwise, made through any medium at his/her studios or elsewhere, and in any and all media now or hereafter known for illustration, promotion, art, editorial, advertising, trade, broadcast or any other purpose whatsoever. I also consent to the use of any printed, broadcast or electronic matter, and any recorded and/or spoken commentary, in conjunction therewith.

I hereby waive any right that I may have to inspect or approve the finished product or products and the advertising copy or other matter that may be used in connection therewith or the use to which it may be applied.

I hereby release, discharge and agree to save harmless Photographer, his/her heirs, legal representatives and assigns, and all persons acting under his/her permissions or authority or those for whom he/she is acting, from any liability by virtue of any blurring, distortion, alteration, optical illusion, or use in composite form, whether intentional or otherwise, that may occur or be produced in the taking of said picture or in any subsequent processing thereof, as well as any publication thereof, including, without limitation, any claims for libel or invasion of privacy.

I hereby warrant that I am of full age and have the right to contract in my own name. I have read the above authorization, release and agreement prior to its execution, and I am fully familiar with the contents thereof. This release shall be binding upon me and my heirs, legal representatives and assigns.

_____   _____
My Signature   **Address**

_____   _____
Date   **Witness Signature**

THE RIGHT OF PRIVACY

Photographs are the usual cases of invasion of privacy, which is the publicizing of information about a person without legitimate and legal purpose.

Violation of someone's privacy rights is not a crime, but a civil offense, or "tort." It is a uniquely American legal creation and did not exist as a legal principle before 1890. Right to privacy legal questions arose after newspapers abandoned using artists' illustrations and began using hand-held plate- and sheet-film cameras, along with the "halftone process" that made it possible to quickly and easily reproduce photographs on the printed page.

The constant threat of a court's interpretation of the concept of invasion of privacy always hangs over a press or PR photographer's activities. The idea of the "right to be left alone" has grown over the years and is susceptible to broad interpretation.

It concerns the protection of the use of a person's name, portrait, image, likeness or picture, sketch, signature, coat of arms and the like – by another – but without the person's consent.

Invasion of privacy involves four basic legal and ethical questions:

- Was the information acquired legally?

- Was there trespassing on private property?

- Did the alleged invasion of privacy occur in the course of covering a legitimate news story?

- Is information about the plaintiff, story or photo, being used to unjustly enrich the writer, photographer or publication? That is, *without consent*. This is an important consideration in advertising.

There are four major types of invasion of privacy suits:

1. **Intrusion.** Upon a person's physical or mental solitude. Two prime areas of concern are home and hospital.

2. **Private Facts.** The biggest problem for photojournalists, and a growing area of invasion of privacy case law. Public support for curbs on photographers is widespread, due to the intrusions of "paparazzi" on celebrities. Photographs showing normally clothed body parts while the subject is on private property, or capturing someone's private moments through a window are examples of invasion of privacy via disclosing "private facts."

3. **False Light.** Fictionalization – mixing facts and fiction. Akin to libel. Photographs can show someone in a false light if they imply acts or relationships that are untrue, even if the photograph was not manipulated in any way.

4. **Appropriation.** Using someone's name or face to sell a commercial product without their permission. This is a problem usually connected with public relations and advertising photographs, because news never is considered commercialization. Photographers should obtain completed release forms to use someone's likeness for monetary gain, even if no money changes hands.

Photojournalists take and publish news photos, but seldom obtain written consent, unless the images may be used later for commercial purposes. For example, a news photo that is reproduced years later in a textbook, long after the news story was "news," could be the basis for an appropriation case.

If a photograph is used for advertising or "for purposes of trade," which includes public relations work, then written consent is the best defense the photographer and his employer can use in case of an invasion of privacy suit.

SUBMITTING DIGITAL PHOTOS

Digital photographs that accompany news releases, features, staff announcements and other e-mailed public relations materials should be included as attachments, not inserted into the body of the e-mail. Information on how to name, caption and attach photographs and other digital images such as maps and illustrations to your PR submittals is contained in Chapter 6 – Sending a News Release.

FILM-BASED PR PHOTOGRAPHY

No doubt about it – Your public relations effort will be greatly hampered if you try to stick with film-based photography. Even if you have a lot of "legacy" materials, such as old prints and negatives, it would be wise to get them into digital form, if only for preservation's sake. Nearly every media operation you will deal with will prefer to receive digital images, and they will not be eager to do the extra work it takes to get a film-based photo on the printed page.

Converting prints, slides and negatives to digital files that are easy to edit, store and e-mail is easy and inexpensive – and it all can done with consumer-level computers, peripherals and software.

However, you may have valid reasons to continue using film. There is a long tradition of news and editorial photography with film cameras. But be warned, the newspaper operations of old, with their photo labs, chemical tanks and halftoning cameras, are extremely scarce even now, and soon will be a thing of the past.

Submitted prints used to be rephotographed to create halftones – little dots of pure black and white or color. Now, prints are scanned and digitized to get to the printed page. Negatives and slides that arrive at a newspaper or magazine also are scanned. The lesson is, you can save the media a lot of work and get better results if you do the digitizing for them.

FILM

In the recent past, most submitted public relations photographs were printed in black-and-white by newspapers. Costly-to-print color photos were generally reserved for the front page. So it followed that much of editorial photography was done on fast black-and-white film, such as Kodak Tri-X 400, a favorite of press photographers in the film era.

Now, it makes no great difference if you submit color negatives, color prints or color slides, because they all are easily converted to black-and-white, if needed, after a publication scans and digitizes them.

The best overall films for film-based PR work are fast color negative films with ISO speeds of 400 to 800. This will allow good exposures in a variety of lighting situations. If your photo shoot is all outdoors in the daytime, use 100- to 200-speed film. Avoid some films, such as Kodachrome, which must be sent to processing centers, often far away.

Slides are delicate, cumbersome and expensive, compared with other types of film and should be avoided for PR photo work, unless specifically requested by a publication. But if you must shoot slides, get slide film that uses the "E-6" development process for best speed and convenience. "Fast photo" places usually do a decent job with E-6 film, although it's often a good idea to stick with the same custom lab that does your prints.

Specify plastic mounts for your slides, not cardboard. If you need multiple slides of the same frame, duplicate slides are inexpensive and almost indistinguishable from the original, although some quality will be lost in the process.

FILM PRINTING

Drugstores, supermarkets and one-hour or overnight labs cater to casual, color print film "snapshooters," who are content with quick, but indifferent, results. Their processes are automated, and the usual product is called "machine prints." These prints often suffer from bad color, poor focus in the enlarging process and are cropped and trimmed shoddily. In short, machine prints will be unacceptable to accompany your news release.

Use machine prints to *view* the photos only, then have the frames of your choice made into custom prints, which benefit from the touch of a skilled human being who ensures that exposure, sharpness and cropping are exactly what you want. A custom printer also can correct some mistakes made in the original negative.

Specify white borders on your prints, not "borderless." The borders leave room for cropping marks, tape mounting and editorial comments without intruding on the image. Ask for glossy prints, not matte or pearl finishes that produce a less-sharp image.

Most publications prefer to receive 4x5, 4x6 or 5x7 size prints, and their production equipment is set up that way. The price per print escalates sharply if you want 8x10s – a waste of money, unless the publication specifically requests that size.

LABELING SLIDES

Before sending out a slide, write in permanent marker on the front, or viewing side, the "slug" of the news release, which is a one- or two-word brief title and your name or organization name. Stick or draw a small red or black dot on the lower left-hand corner. This "thumb spot" will help in projecting or duplicating the slide correctly.

Under the frame window, write a brief name for the slide. This "frame title" also will be referenced on the printed sheet that contains your captions.

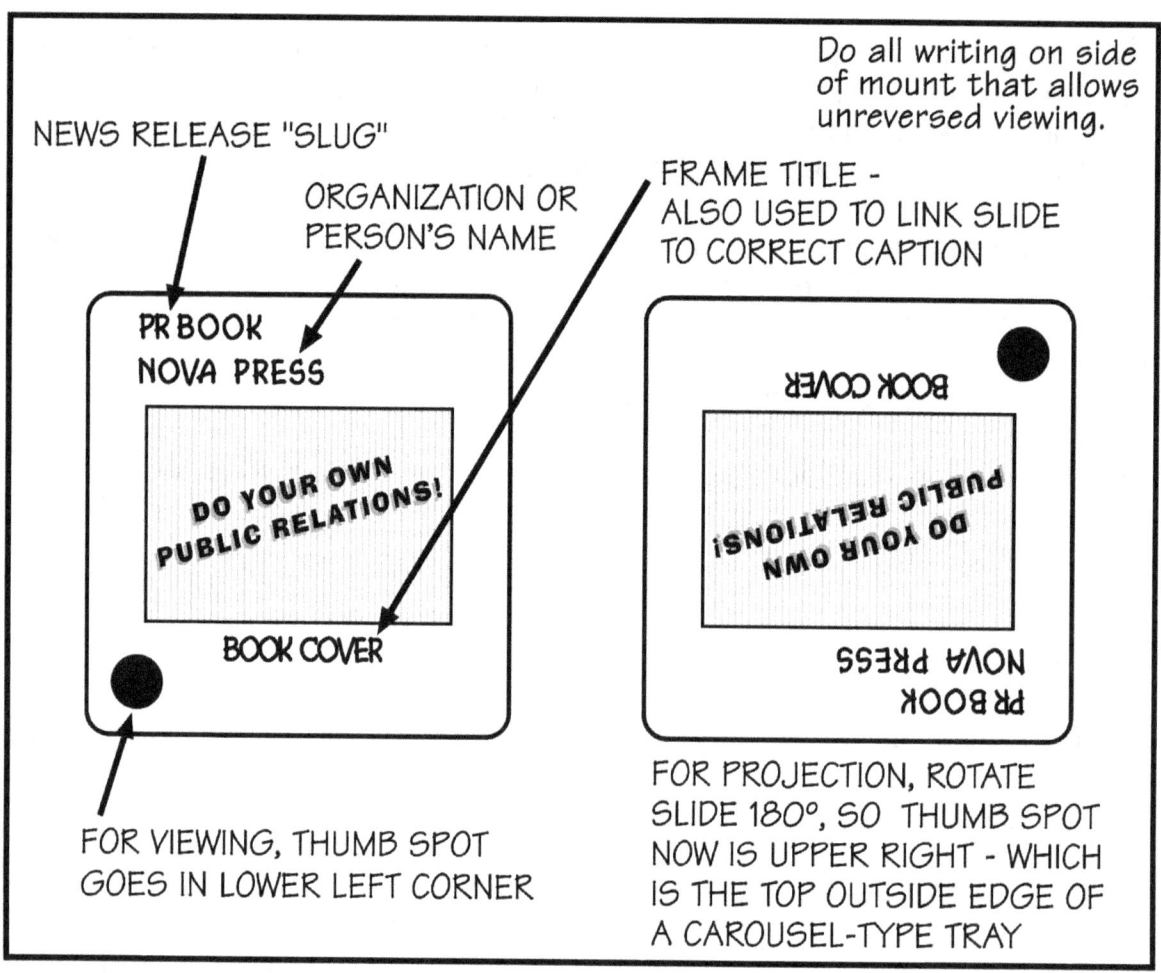

SLIDE SLEEVES AND CAPTION SHEETS

Don't leave slides loose – They are easily scratched and misplaced. Put the slides for your PR submittal in clear vinyl slide sleeves, available at office supply stores and photo shops. If you're sending just a few slides, cut the slide sleeve so it's no larger than necessary.

Print all your captions on letter-size paper, clearly linking each caption to its corresponding frame title. Staple the caption sheet(s) to the clear slide sleeve, so the captions and the slides cannot become separated.

Chapter 10: Photographs

SENDING NEGATIVES AND CAPTIONS

This never is a good idea. Publications often promise to take good care of your negatives, but accidents happen. And negatives are often-priceless and irreplaceable original images that should not leave your possession. Be prepared to find your negatives returned with fingerprints, scratches and other calamities.

If you *must* submit negatives to the tender mercies of the media, first have them scanned to digital or photographically copied. Roll-film negatives, such as 35mm frames, most often are in strips of two to six frames, cut from the original continuous roll. These strips should be protected in clear vinyl negative-holder sleeves. The same kind of sleeves should be used to send the negatives. Like the sleeves for slides, the negative holders can be cut down to a smaller size – depending on how many negatives you're sending – and stapled to the printed caption sheet.

On your captions that are linked to negatives, reference the frame number, which is an integral part of the film. For example,

```
Frame 22:
Principal Mary Smith welcomes students to the new
library at Washington Elementary School during a
ribbon-cutting ceremony Friday.
Photo courtesy School District No. 12.
```

SENDING PRINTS AND CAPTIONS

Because they're delicate, hard to handle and require a lot of work on the part of publishers before they're ready for printing, slides and negatives always should take a distant back seat to prints as the preferred film-based media for your PR submittals. Prints can be reproduced in volume for low cost, and are more easily viewed and scanned than slides or negatives. Prints also can be stored flat without much risk of damage, ready to be used.

The illustration on the following page shows a method for attaching a print to a caption in a way that reduces the chance the two items will become separated.

Note the print is not glued to the caption page, but attached by clear tape on the top edge only. The print/caption combination is then stapled behind the page(s) of your news release, PR feature or other submittal. Use a separate caption page for each print.

A FINAL WORD ON FILM-BASED PR PHOTOGRAPHY:

Film is more complicated, expensive, time-consuming, difficult to handle and store, prone to mistakes and less accepted by most media than digital image files. With film, you are much more dependent on outside services, and likely will end up with lower-quality results.

Avoid film if at all possible.

METHOD FOR ATTACHING PRINTS AND CAPTIONS

LETTER-SIZE
WHITE PAPER

STAPLE BEHIND
NEWS RELEASE
AT UPPER LEFT

CONTACTS AND
CAPTION ABOVE
PHOTOGRAPH

Sept. 12, 2007
FOR IMMEDIATE RELEASE

Contact:
Peter Smith, 555-7777

PETE'S GOLF CARS NEW LOCATION GRAND OPENING –

Owner Peter M. Smith greets customers at the September
12 grand opening of his newest golf car retail and
service center, at 5555 N. Park Vista Lane in Sierra
Vista. It is the third location for Pete's Golf Cars,
Inc., which also has locations in Tucson and Green
Valley. Smith said sales were expected to top $1 million
this year.

TAPE IN TWO PLACES ON
TOP EDGE OF PHOTO.
AVOID TAPING IN
IMAGE AREA.

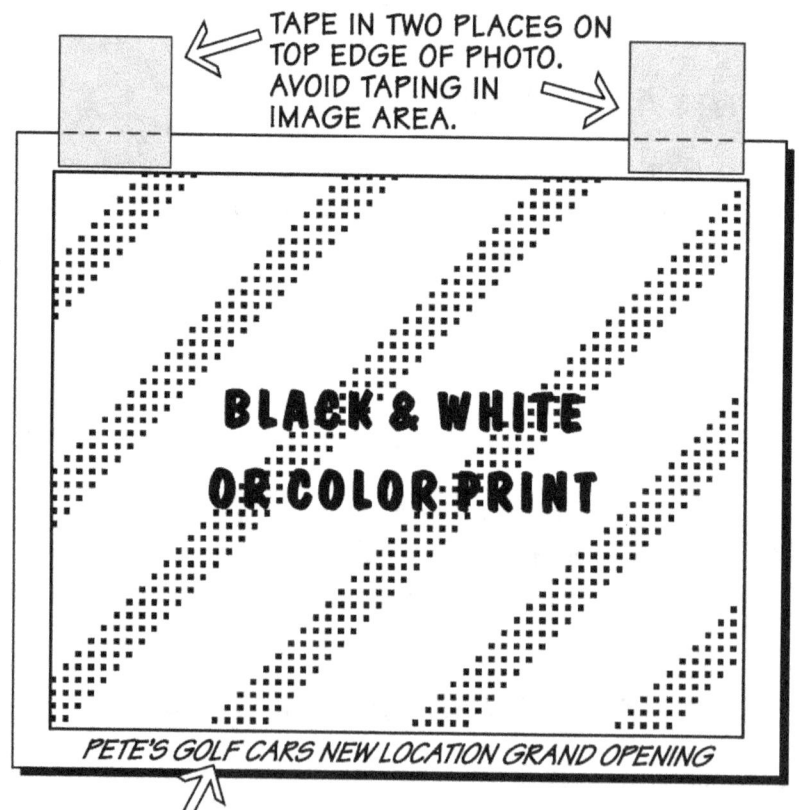

PETE'S GOLF CARS NEW LOCATION GRAND OPENING

PRINT TITLE OF PHOTO
IN WHITE BORDER AREA

CHAPTER 11
<u>MEDIA KITS</u>

WHAT ARE MEDIA KITS?

Media kits – also called "press kits" – are folders, binders or envelopes that bring together many of the items described in preceding chapters. They are assembled to give the media a comprehensive view of your organization or event, and oftentimes are distributed with a news release, to serve as background information. They help journalists produce an accurate story and saves a lot of time for them, which greatly improves the chances of your public relations story being accepted.

Media kits can be "evergreen" – that is, containing information that will not be outdated soon. The kits can be kept on the shelf until you have something newsworthy, then a fresh news release can be added and the kits sent out.

WHAT GOES INTO A MEDIA KIT?

- News releases
- Fact Sheets
- Staff announcements
- Photographic prints and captions
- Pre-generated "evergreen" feature articles
- Brochures and catalogs
- Copies of published articles (clippings) about your organization
- Illustrations and maps
- Financial statements
- Biographical material such as resumes
- Copies of licenses and awards
- Schedules, timelines and calendars of events
- "Backgrounders" or briefing papers – a type of news release with in-depth information about an organization or event
- Videos – on VHS tape or DVD
- CDs or DVDs with any or all of the items above. The entire media kit can be in this form, but include some hard copy material with it

SIMPLE IS BETTER

You don't have to spend a fortune to obtain a professional-looking media kit that represents your organization well. Inexpensive, two-pocket folders imprinted with a logo and basic information such as addresses and telephone numbers are good vehicles to carry media kits. I have seen media kits from some very large and well-heeled organizations that follow this exact arrangement.

The news release is inserted into the left-hand pocket, on top of other items on that side, where it will be noticed and read first. The right-side pocket can contain supporting material, and is a good spot to put photographs.

If possible, staple all related material together, such as all the pages of a feature story, so they won't be lost or disorganized when taken out of the folder or envelope.

If you are including photographs or other graphical material in your press kit, place them topmost in the right-side pocket, where it will attract attention and lure the reader into taking it out and looking it over. Right-side "gray" text-type material, such as fact sheets or feature articles, always should be behind the photos and graphics.

UPDATE YOUR MEDIA KIT OFTEN

A few complete media kits should be kept on hand, ready to hand out on a minute's notice. A plain white paper strip should be inserted into each completed media kit folder, sticking out at the top, with the date the kit was assembled or updated. This simple system will help prevent distributing out-of-date media kits.

The best way to keep your media kit organized and useful is to keep the various elements of it in separate slots of a cabinet or collator. The slots can be labeled, "Fact Sheet," "Staff," "Sept. 2009 newspaper story," etc.

Everyone in the organization should be aware of the media kit and what's in it, so they can alert the persons responsible for upkeep of the kit when changes may be needed. Spend a few bucks and make sure everyone has their own copy of the media kit.

DON'T BUY A DINOSAUR

Many small businesses and organizations fall into the trap of shelling out a lot of money to produce a glossy brochure that quickly becomes obsolete or is distributed poorly, leaving thousands of useless copies laying around, gathering dust.

A brochure is a poor media kit, but a well-planned media kit makes a serviceable brochure – one that can be easily updated at low cost. And by all means – If you have some glossy material that's current, such as a current brochure or catalog, pop it in the media kit.

WHEN DO YOU SEND OUT THE MEDIA KIT?

Your media kit should be inexpensive enough to produce that you won't have to wince at sending out sufficient copies to cover your public relations needs. Keeping the cost of the media kit down makes it easier to send out lots of copies when appropriate.

Keep a list of whom you've sent media kits to, and review it regularly to cull out dead ends, unresponsive persons, defunct organizations and the like. This list of media kit recipients should be based on the media list discussed in Chapter 6 – Sending a News Release, but probably will have its own unique set of contacts.

Your most important media contacts – local newspapers, radio and television; industry publications; and the chamber of commerce – should get new kits after you have made enough changes to make their old versions undesirable, or annually, whichever comes first.

It's very likely your media kit has been thrown out long ago to make room in the newsroom for other piles of paper, so you have to keep supplying new ones. If nothing else, this will remind them that you're still out there

A media kit often accompanies a news release, but not always. News releases should be sent by themselves to journalists if you already have provided a media kit to them. A media kit should go along with a news release if the release is sent to a fresh media target, such as a new radio station or startup publication.

WHO GETS THE MEDIA KIT?

A good media kit is useful for other things than supplying information to the media: It can help sell your services the same way an advertisement does. This greatly increases the number of possible recipients for your kit, and increases its value as both a public relations tool and a marketing resource. Consider sending a media kit to:

- Local media – newspapers, radio and TV stations, magazines
- Your employees
- Your business contacts
- Current customers
- Potential customers
- Your local chambers of commerce
- Economic development organizations, both public and private
- Family and friends
- Anyone that may have an opportunity to pass it on to someone useful

CHAPTER 12
OTHER MEDIA-CONTACT METHODS

OTHER METHODS ARE AVAILABLE

E-mailed or hard copy news releases, staff announcements, features and media kits are a good way to get your message to journalists, but other appropriate methods are available. Most of them require more time, money and personal involvement than simply e-mailing material to an address.

WHY TRY OTHER METHODS?

Editors and reporters get lots of e-mails and fat envelopes every day. Most of them are of no interest to the media, but even submittals with high news interest may get overlooked in the avalanche of stuff.

Your public relations material may need an extra reminder or special presentation to gain the attention of an editor. Most business telephone calls fail on the first try to connect the caller with the person they're trying to reach, so lots of attempts often are necessary to make contact and accomplish something. So it is with PR submittals.

THE PERSONAL TOUCH

It's much easier for the media to reject a public relations effort by "remote control" – deleting or throwing away unsolicited stuff without ever speaking to the person who sent it. For this reason, it's always a good idea to follow-up your submittals with a telephone call the next day to help sell the item. If you have a pleasant, persuasive personality, so much the better.

Phone calls – or face-to-face meetings for that matter – will put a human face on your PR dealings and will exert some gentle pressure on your target media to cooperate. But don't call to complain; call to convince.

TELEPHONE CALLS

The old-fashioned phone call still has its uses. Once you've made a connection to the person you want to reach, it's immediate, interactive – and you're guaranteed at least 10 to 20 seconds to make your point.

Don't abuse this option. Reserve your media telephone calls for the times it really matters to push your information.

THANK-YOUs

Journalists rarely get praise from the community. When they do hear from their audience, it's almost always a complaint, which has little or no effect on reporters and editors. They will, however, appreciate and remember a call from you sincerely thanking them for covering your event or placing your public relations submittal.

You need to establish a good working relationship with the media for effective publicity. Letting them know you're grateful for what they do will pay off in the long run.

PRESS LUNCHEONS

Set up a lunch meeting with a local journalist you'd like to establish a better relationship with. It's done all the time for PR purposes, but don't make this noontime meeting into a 60-minute sales pitch. Keep it light and conversational; ask as many questions as you receive. Don't invite more than one journalist to lunch at one time, even if they're coworkers.

Work in details about your company or organization only after a friendly basis has been established. Let the journalist know you're favorably inclined to the press and eager to cooperate with their need for information.

Note: When the bill comes, don't automatically take charge and offer to pay for everything – This could be interpreted as a cheap bribe. Give the journalist the opportunity to cover their portion of the meal or the tip, and don't refuse their money if it's offered. If they don't bring out their wallet within a minute or two or ask if they can pay for themselves, then you can assume they're comfortable with you paying the bill.

NEWS CONFERENCES

Often, an organization will want to make an *event* of releasing their news and hold a news conference. These are open meetings where a spokesperson addresses an audience and usually is available for questions. There can be more than one speaker. Displays, printed material handouts, projected material or product samples/demonstrations may be used.

News conferences should be reserved for big announcements that will greatly affect the community, local business or your industry. They're announced in advance via a news release or a direct telephone call to the media. Prior to the news conference, a news release should give some idea of what it is about, and distributing media kits or other handouts at the conference is common practice.

News conferences should be handled by your PR specialist, and include someone in your organization directly involved with the news, such as a company officer, who has the knowledge and authority to answer questions. Of course, some talent as a public speaker is desirable. Follow the basic rules of news releases in the presentation – Keep it short, avoid jargon, and be honest and accurate.

NETWORKING

Effective contacts with the media can be made *indirectly* by getting more involved in activities that attract favorable attention, or already have a strong connection to the journalists you want to reach.

Business, service and fraternal clubs always are well-connected to local radio and TV stations and newspapers. Because these organizations generally benefit the community and do good works, they have memberships full of influential people who have good relations with the media.

Join up, contribute and take advantage of the public relations benefits of involvement with the local Rotary, Elks, chamber of commerce, Boy Scouts, Ducks Unlimited, church group, sports or hobby club, or similar circle that enjoys positive press. You'll find many opportunities to piggyback your own PR efforts with that of the group, and you'll widen the circle of interest in your news.

This kind of networking works well on the local level, and involvement in state, national and international business and professional organizations also can work to the same advantage, albeit in a much larger, more diffuse venue. These big groups usually have professional PR specialists and materials that could prove to be a valuable asset to your own efforts.

EDITORIAL ADVERTISING

If you can't get your news release or feature accepted by a newspaper, consider paid placement. This involves paying for the space, just like placing a display ad. The difference is that the piece is formatted to look like a news story, with the same font and column layout as the rest of the newspaper. The paper likely will put a small notice at the beginning or end of the story, letting readers know it was a paid piece and not the product of the paper's own editorial staff.

REGULAR COLUMNS

Newspapers, magazines and Web sites often run columns on a regular basis written by business people and others with specialized knowledge – gardening, healthcare, local history, pets, technical matters and the like. The key to successful acceptance of the PR-based column is that it provides some benefit to the readers beyond entertainment. The contributor typically is not paid.

This is a "win/win" situation for everyone concerned. The publication gets a free column that's helpful and interesting to readers, and the writer gets favorable public relations exposure, with the sole cost being the time it took to produce the piece.

PHOTO OPPORTUNITIES

If your public relations news is photogenic, the media will appreciate the chance to show up and get some eye-catching images via photos or video. Photos are a low-cost way for newspapers and other publications to fill their pages. TV news departments need a lot of footage to produce to original broadcasts three or four times a day.

"Photo ops" can be announced by news release. Give the media four or five days advance notice. Telephone calls also work, especially if the photo op is unexpected. One-day notice, or even less, is OK if longer lead times are not possible. Short notice can even work to your advantage, as this can make the photo op seem more "newsy."

WEB SITES

If you have a Web site, it can be used to post news releases and every kind of information on you or your operation. Your Web site can be referenced on hard copy PR submittals, and live links to it posted in e-mails, Word documents, photo captions, etc.

The downside of putting a lot of information on a Web site is that it must be maintained: Old or incorrect stuff must be regularly purged, and new stuff must be posted in a timely manner. It should be pointed out that most business Web sites are designed and maintained by third-party specialists who charge – usually a lot – by the hour for their services, which drives up the cost of conducting public relations this way.

If you're trying to do your own PR, make sure you have the time, money and commitment to keep a proper Web site before embarking on this method of communication.

SOCIAL AND BUSINESS NETWORKS ON THE INTERNET

Facebook, its copycats and competitors, along with various business and professional social networks, are here to stay. It's relatively easy to establish a presence on any of these, and the price – usually free – is right. However, do not think a social network page will accomplish your PR goals: You need a more professional and direct link to the media than just referring to your page in an ad or a news release and asking the world to "like" you.

So go ahead and set up a page for your business or organization. Just remember, like a Web site, this is one more thing you have to maintain regularly.

BLOGS

Not a good idea. Blogs are everywhere, and most of them are read by just a handful of the author's friends. The typical blog is full of opinion, which is not at all what good PR should be about. Save your effort for better things.

INTERNET BULLETIN BOARDS

The Internet now is the preferred way to get information, shouldering aside most traditional sources, from the local grapevine to the network evening news. People don't rely on the journalism pros so much anymore, and will form opinions based on what they see on Web sites, bulletin boards, discussion groups, live chat and blogs.

There's a lot of bogus info masquerading as fact floating around in cyberspace. Rumor, innuendo and lies never have had such fertile ground, making the Information Superhighway a media Wild West. The pervasive anonymity of the Internet makes it easy to post almost anything without much fear of discovery or consequences.

Still, no competent in-house PR effort would be complete without making use of this unregulated – and free – "new media" venue that shapes public opinion and perceptions perhaps more than anything else, including national news organizations.

Go ahead and post favorable comments about your business or organization on a bulletin board or discussion forum. Encourage employees and friends to do the same. Initiate or steer positive discussion toward your operation and use it to bolster public opinion.

There's nothing illegal about self-posting good comments – and nothing unethical, as long as you don't misrepresent yourself as being someone you aren't. Stick to being anonymous.

GOOD WORKS

Actively seek out opportunities to contribute to the community in ways that will be of interest to the media. Help out a needy family; fund a modest scholarship; donate your product or service. Get people from your operation out to clean up a stretch of roadside or a park.

The very nature of charitable activities and efforts to publicize gives them a leg up on acceptance by the media.

Try to stand out from the crowd, performing good works that are exclusively yours. This not only makes you all the more prominent in any resulting press coverage, but makes it much easier to handle as a public relations project. You are in charge of informing the media, and will not have to depend on someone else to do a good job of PR.

It may *seem* desirable at first glance to be in a public relations pool along with others to accomplish some kindness, but all you may end up with is a tiny line in a "thank-you" ad, if that. Charitable undertakings and contributions under the banner of another organization are not ideal for PR purposes. Any press coverage will feature that organization, not yours.

Good works, at least as far as PR is concerned, is generally best done unilaterally.

SPONSORSHIPS

Not just supporting sports teams, but academic teams or supplies or travel for a worthy individual competitor. When you help outfit a dozen kids, you're gaining not only 12 little mobile billboards with your name and logo, but a host of parents, relatives and friends abounding with gratitude and good will toward their sponsor. Good will that will resonate and expand throughout the community. This is the essence of good PR.

Anyone you sponsor should agree, in writing, that you may publicize your support of them.

SPEAKER'S BUREAUS

A little checking around in your area will uncover a way to connect with venues – schools, business organizations, clubs, luncheon gatherings, special events – that are looking for speakers. Sometimes called "speaker's bureaus," these groups specialize in generating rosters of willing people able to deliver talks on topics they're knowledgeable about.

Community involvement as a speaker guarantees you an audience and an opportunity to make a good impression face-to-face. If you also can give people something to take home after the talk is over – brochures, product samples, logo pens – the impression will linger.

SOME BAD IDEAS:

Following are a few media-contact methods of dubious value, yet they're still around.

FAXED NEWS RELEASES

Facsimile telephone transmission of news releases enjoyed a brief heyday, beginning in the late 1980s, but it's no longer such a great idea. Journalists already are inundated with news releases through their e-mail and postal mail, and do not care to have their telephone lines, fax machines, fax paper and trash basket space used up by unwanted news releases.

As if that weren't enough, fax transmissions lose image quality, particularly on photographs and graphics with gradient tones, and generally leave a bad impression. Stick to e-mail.

VIDEO NEWS RELEASES

Video news releases, or VNRs, are short "canned" video productions that look like news footage, but are supplied by businesses and organizations to highlight something newsworthy, exactly like a printed news release. They usually have a host or a "reporter," actually a company spokesperson, who introduces the piece, provides voice-over commentary and conducts interviews. Total length typically is from three minutes – about the length of a piece on the evening news – to a half-hour or more.

This is a job best left to a professional video production company. VNRs are relatively expensive to produce and often have short shelf-lives because changes in the organization or its products and services make them obsolete quickly. Television news departments won't run VNRs, but may use portions from them to flesh out a story on the same topic.

VNRs used to be submitted on VHS videotape, but changes in technology now have most of them on DVDs or as e-mailed video files. Unless you have captive audiences in mind or journalists with a lot of time on their hands, there's probably not a very big market for video news releases.

MULTIPLE TELEPHONE CALLS

There's a line between aggressive self-promotion and simply being a pest, and repeatedly calling an editor to push a public relations item crosses it. *One* call is good – Your PR stuff might have gotten lost in the daily incoming pile, or maybe it just needed a little reminder to get placed.

But calling again – or again and again – won't do any good, and probably will be counterproductive. Leave it alone and move on to new and better things.

COMPLAINING

Reporters and editors get complaints all day long. Probably more in a week than most people hear in a year. They're used to it, and criticism bounces off their thick skin.

Journalists need "hard bark" to do their job: What they do often upsets and offends thousands of people every day, and they can't let it affect their reporting. For this reason, your peevish complaint about a publication not running your PR item – or running it too small or on a back page – will fall on deaf ears.

In short, don't bother to complain, unless you need to see a serious error corrected.

WHY THE PRESS IS UNIQUE

Journalists have long enjoyed a unique position in our society. The "fourth estate" acts as an extragovernmental check on politicians and the military, guards the public trust, advises consumers, champions underdogs and performs a host of useful functions in society.

The media has a lot of real power, and although most reporters usually are not lavishly paid for their work, they are fairly resistant to corruption, outside influence and threats. For example, it's rare to see a reporter in this country hurt or killed by organized crime or gangs, for fear of the intense media reaction and scrutiny such an action would provoke.

An old journalistic maxim goes, "You don't mess with people who buy ink by the barrel."

Accounts seldom surface about a reporter or reviewer who took payoffs to produce a favorable story. To offer a bribe or perk to a reporter to kill or change a story is a risky ploy.

Even before the Bill of Rights, lawmakers in what was to become the United States recognized the value of an independent press. Since the nation's founding, a body of law has been established to protect reporters and news organizations.

But because of their protected status and power to influence, media types can seem arrogant and abrupt to outsiders. And some reporters routinely cross the line of objectivity and let their own political or personal agendas color their product. Consequently, the public perception of a biased press is widespread today and probably here to stay.

FOSTER YOUR GOOD REPUTATION

Part of the job of a public relations professional is to keep on the good side of the media and avoid making enemies of the very people they depend on for favorable publicity. PR types establish relationships with reporters, columnists, editors and the like, and try to build reputations for honesty and fair dealing.

As your own public relations representative, this is now part of your job.

A good reputation will help sell your public relations materials to the media as much as anything else described in this book. If your designated media-contact person has a prickly, easily offended personality or is hypersensitive to criticism, find someone else to do the work, because you soon will have an enemy down at the local newspaper – an enemy with the power to swat down your PR efforts with a mouse click on the "delete" button.

RULES OF DEALING WITH THE MEDIA

It can't be stressed too much: The media wants your legitimately useful and newsy public relations material to help fill the pages of copy and hours of broadcast they must push out the door every day. But they won't put up with bad behavior or deal with people who cross the line between earnestly seeking good publicity and outright hucksterism.

Take the following rules to heart and make them part of your standard operating procedures for public relations.

Stick to the truth

Of course, avoid outright deception – but failing to disclose or acknowledge bad news or embarrassing facts until confronted with "smoking gun" evidence by a reporter will serve you poorly in the media and make even your truthful statements suspect. Reporters deal with people who have something to hide on a daily basis, and they are skilled at recognizing half-truths and meaningless mumbo-jumbo.

"Stonewalling" is the kiss of death

Make yourself available to the press, particularly in a crisis situation. If you don't make the effort to answer reasonable questions from reporters, return their calls and act responsibly, it surely will boomerang back on you and your organization.

Answer media telephone queries promptly

Journalists are driven by deadlines. Recognizing their needs and the importance of making the next edition or broadcast will help you immensely in dealing with reporters and editors.

Don't form a sour view of the media based on a few bad experiences

Every business has some bad apples, and even the friendliest reporters can be overly brusque or arrogant at times. If you feel you were treated poorly by a particular reporter or editor, give them a second chance. If it becomes apparent there really is an attitude problem, try a different reporter. If you have no alternate person at that particular media operation to get your material run, then just live with it. Eventually, there will be staff turnover or they will need to contact *you* for a story. At that point, forget about the past incidents and move forward with your public relations mission.

Avoid "off the record" statements

Loose lips sink ships – and reputations. Always assume you will be quoted and be careful and accurate when making statements. Don't think that a verbal arrangement with a reporter to not repeat whatever scurrilous thing you're about to say constitutes an ironclad contract. Quash any inner desire to be a big mouth and stick to the facts and the story at hand.

Don't combine news releases with advertising or editorial items:

Public relations is not advertising, and failing to appreciate this will damage your PR efforts. Even if your news release is tied to a sale or promotion, keep the two worlds of journalism and advertising separate.

Leverage your advertising relationship

Media people always have potential ad sales in mind – that's what keeps them in the black. If your business is one that advertises, you should establish an ongoing relationship with a newspaper, radio station or other media outlet by buying some ads. This can help push your public relations materials: You will be a familiar face, and they will want to keep you happy. Of course, most media types will deny this type of subtle influence, but it exists.

Don't overplay your news item - avoid hyperbole

Let the value of your news sell itself. It's much better to appear as a humble and understated professional than a used car salesman. Avoid terms like "major story," "big news," "important development" and "groundbreaking product" when you contact journalists with your PR information.

Don't play favorites or discriminate with the press

If you have an ax to grind with someone down at the local newspaper or an old buddy at the radio station, don't let this influence how you send out news releases or respond to calls. Be evenhanded in your distribution of information and don't try to curry favor by guaranteeing "exclusive" rights to your story. It will backfire in short order.

Don't complain of minor misprints, errors or misquotes

You might care, but nobody else does, including the readers and viewers. Let this sleeping dog doze.

Don't complain if a story ends up on a back page or is not run

Print and broadcast media have no obligation to play up your public relations story, or even to run it at all. You're doing them a favor by supplying something of interest; they're doing you a favor by giving it consideration. Your story may get pushed aside on a busy news day by more important items or get dumped because the precious page space or airtime was taken up by advertising. But the best reason to not complain is it won't do any good, and could hurt your relationship with the media.

Don't be afraid to make follow-up calls

If your PR news doesn't appear, it's OK to call the media and ask what happened. Just don't be annoyed by the answer. You might even learn something valuable to apply to your next public relations submittal.

Don't go over a reporter's head to complain to the editor

This is a pointless, futile practice and as good a way as any to make enemies down at the newspaper or radio station. If there was a problem with your story, try to deal in a friendly way with the reporter who handled your story. They will appreciate your good attitude and probably look forward to your next contact.

Don't tolerate errors of fact

This isn't a complaint: Errors of fact in a story – real errors and not just minor details – should be pointed out and corrected. So go ahead and make that call. If the media makes an error of fact mistake when they run your information, let them know about it and ask for a correction. Corrections are run all the time, and they lessen the media's legal liability.

Try to be as helpful with bad news as well as good
Just because you don't like the direction of a story involving you or your organization, that's no reason to deep-six your relationship with the reporter. Contrary to what many people think, reporters usually don't relish holding a grudge against a newsmaker.

"Thank you" is good as gold
Reporters and editors are accustomed to getting complaints all day, every day, so it's a ray of sunshine when someone calls up and thanks them for a story. They will remember you as someone who made their day.

How about lunch?
Suggest a lunch meeting to a reporter or other media type with whom you want to discuss your public relations topic. The typical lunch hour likely will result in you getting more "face time" with the reporter than most venues. This is strictly a business lunch, not a bribe. As covered in Chapter 12, don't offer in advance to pay, but graciously offer to cover the tab when the bill arrives. The other party always has the option to turn down your suggestion and pay their portion of the bill and tip. Stick to lunch: Dinner crosses that tricky line between professionalism and payola.

Understand the tension between business and the media
Both are suspicious of one another, based on decades of business trying to conceal bad news and journalists rooting it out. It is your job to try to create and maintain good relationships with the media on a person-by-person basis. Make it your practice to do your own public relations without an adversarial approach to the media.

Don't isolate knowledgeable personnel from the media
While reporters appreciate access to executives and owners, they also need to talk to lower-echelon people who have first-hand experience with the topic. Give your staff some direction and trust them to do the right thing with the media.

Don't overlook radio
There are a lot more radio stations than television stations, and many of them cater to locally produced programming and community news. It may not seem as glamorous or effective as TV, but you stand a good chance of getting 10 times the air time on radio. Daytime radio also has a huge audience – and people don't watch TV in their cars.

Don't get upset if nothing results from your news release
Most news releases end up in the trash. And yes, some do not get a fair shake from jaded media people. Keep trying and be patient.

Increase your interest-factor by saying something memorable
In the short time you have to speak or be interviewed, try for an interesting quote. If it's good, with real content and interest, it will end up in the published or broadcast story. Think about this well ahead of time and try out a few sound bites or punchy lines on coworkers or your family. Use their feedback and remember: You're probably not as witty as you think.

Use "no comment" wisely

There are lots of legitimate reasons to answer "no comment" to a journalist's question: Ongoing or pending litigation; medical or employee privacy; minors involved; or you just don't know the answer. It's not a cop-out and it's not like taking the Fifth in a trial. It would be a very bad thing if you legally compromised yourself or someone else by revealing privileged information or by engaging in speculation and guesswork.

If possible, explain why you can't comment as part of your answer. And if you can't comment because it would expose you to criminal or civil charges, just keep quiet and call your lawyer.

Be flexible -- don't stick to an old, bad story if the situation changes

If you were wrong in previous comments, admit it. It shows you've been doing your homework and are open to other facts and opinions. Be prepared to explain why you changed your mind.

THE GOLDEN RULE APPLIES

Your relationship with the media is no different than other personal or business relationships you have. Honestly earns big rewards and helps ensure longevity; lies will be found out and will quickly destroy even the best connection.

And, while you may feel that you're not getting as good as you give from the media, keep your eye on the greater good of fostering positive public awareness through good public relations and be a pro about it.

Above all, the Golden Rule still applies: Treat others – even reporters – like you'd want to be treated.

WHAT IS CRISIS MANAGEMENT?

"Crisis management" or "crisis communications" refers to dealing with a potentially damaging public relations problem, before, during and after it occurs.

It's a service offered by PR professionals as part of a complete public relations plan. They will study your operation, plan in advance for a crisis and deal with the media and the public if it occurs. Agency spokespersons will convey your statements to reporters and insulate you from the possible unpleasantness.

Crisis management by PR representatives generally is disliked by reporters because it stands between them and firsthand knowledge: They can't get to the people they really want to talk to and question them directly.

A business or organization that opts to do its own public relations and has a crisis communications plan in place is in a good position: It can react quickly in a crisis with in-house talent at low expense and can gratify the media by providing direct access to responsible people with dependable knowledge.

WHAT CONSTITUTES A PUBLIC RELATIONS 'CRISIS?'

In the public relations sense, a crisis is any situation – whether or not it's your fault – that creates widespread negative publicity with the potential to deal serious damage to your reputation and financial bottom line.

In some cases, bad press can be terminal – It may create a public image of your business or organization that's so unfavorable and enduring, you never will regain the public's trust and bounce back to your former status.

THE FOUR STAGES OF A PUBLIC RELATIONS CRISIS

Like most personal disasters, an evolving PR crisis takes its victims through a quartet of distinct stages before they rally themselves to deal with it.

First, there's *anger* – "How dare the media broadcast this story!" Then comes *denial* – "This whole thing will blow over in a few weeks and we'll be back to normal." *Depression* is next – "The bad news didn't just disappear, public opinion is negative and the organization is suffering from it." Then, the fourth and final stage, *anxiety* appears – "How much damage to our reputation will result from this? What if this bad publicity is here to stay? What can we do about it?"

The one good thing about the *anxiety* stage is that the organization finally is ready to commit to facing the problem and tackling the public relations issues involved. This commitment involves a willingness to spend the time and money necessary to understand the root cause of the bad publicity and learn how to reverse the tide of public opinion.

Every business or organization is liable to suffer a public relations crisis at some time – and all of them should have a PR crisis management plan in place.

ARE YOU CRISIS-PRONE?

Public relations crises are not the exclusive realm of big corporations and prominent politicians. Nearly everyone reading this book has a potential PR crisis waiting to happen, although the danger may not be apparent. Do you have a business or organization that is:

- **Prone to accidents or emergencies?**
    - chemical plant, manufacturing, transportation, construction, recreation
- **Susceptible to lawsuits?**
    - professional service, medical provider, restaurant, sports, retailer
- **In the public eye?**
    - government agency, politician, charity, promoter
- **Under government regulation and scrutiny?**
    - stockbroker, developer, manufacturer, food processor
- **Vulnerable to employee crime?**
    - bank, security, hotel, store, public trust
- **At nature's mercy?**
    - agribusiness, construction, outdoor events
- **At the mercy of others higher up?**
    - franchise, local branch of parent organization
- **New?**
    - start-up operation, new product or service, unproven track record
- **Declining?**
    - financial and labor problems, competition, out of vogue
- **A social outsider?**
    - unpopular or fringe political, religious or other beliefs
- **Heir to a bad reputation?**
    - a history of problems and bad press

You probably identified with two or more of the broad categories above. In some of them, potential legal liability is closely linked to potential public relations problems. In others, factors that can turn public opinion to your disadvantage are at work.

TYPES OF PUBLIC RELATIONS CRISES

A public relations crisis is, above all, a *public* crisis, played out in the open for all to see. A PR crisis begins with a regular crisis – not necessarily human-caused – that's been mishandled and exacerbated by poor communications and a hostile public.

Many crisis situations are well-managed and do not linger in the public eye. They're dealt with and they go away, sometimes so quickly it's as if they never happened.

A crisis can be unintentional, such as an act of nature, or intentional – employee crime, company negligence and the like.

Act of nature are events over which you have no control – an airplane crash, a fire, a flood. These things just happen, and they're usually handled effectively by telling the truth. But organizations can create PR crises out of these seemingly straightforward situations by ill-conceived efforts at "spin," clumsy cover-ups and ineffective communication.

Allowing a public relations crisis to grow from an unintentional crisis is a largely avoidable situation. When you have a crisis communication plan in place and understand the value of public relations, the damage can be minimized or nipped in the bud.

A PR crisis also can suddenly surface from a problem that's been festering for years – put on the back burner by management in a state of denial – until something puts it in the public eye and reporters begin to ask questions.

Certain types of public figures, such as entertainers, politicians and wealthy socialites, enjoy an attitude of low expectations from the public and even benefit from bad behavior that would ruin a small business. Following a gaffe and the ensuing firestorm of negative publicity, the typical celebrity issues an apology, meets with representatives of victim groups, and finally appears on late-night TV to joke about the matter.

"Any publicity is good publicity" works for them, but not for the rest of us.

THE THREE ESSENTIALS OF CRISIS MANAGEMENT

1. **Have a crisis communications plan prepared in advance.**

2. **Designate a single spokesperson to develop and implement your plan and deal with the media.**

3. **Make sure everyone in your organization knows their role in a crisis.**

YOUR CRISIS COMMUNICATIONS PLAN

To ensure effective handling of press relations during an emergency, the person responsible for public relations in your organization should prepare in advance a carefully considered crisis communication plan. Everyone in the organization should take the plan seriously and be ready to do their part during a crisis.

"Brainstorming" sessions can give direction to a crisis communication plan. Think about the worst imaginable situations in which the organization might find itself. You may be surprised what turns up – criminal indictment, consumer class-action lawsuit, sex scandal, whistleblower revelations, embezzlement. Large corporations and government agencies often postulate "worst-case" scenarios and run simulations to test their preparedness.

Then again, many operations never think in terms of a crisis communications plan – and they eventually regret it.

YOUR CRISIS COMMUNICATION SPOKESPERON

Ideally, your crisis spokesperson will be the same person as your regular in-house public relations specialist. The particular qualities of this person that made them a good PR representative should also come into play during a crisis.

Use a single PR spokesperson – This will put forward a familiar face to the media and avoids disseminating contradictory information to the media from multiple sources in your organization. The spokesperson also should have the responsibility and authority to develop and implement your crisis communication plan and have the full support and trust of management.

Your public relations crisis spokesperson should:

- Be well-organized
- Be able to respond quickly to media needs
- Be knowledgeable about the organization and its services
- Be loyal and enthusiastic
- Be an effective written and oral communicator
- Be able to actively lead and direct a conversation
- Be Friendly
- Project a calm, confident, positive image
- Communicate an honest, consistent, plausible message
- Be able to cultivate and maintain a good relationship with the media

Your spokesperson should have easy access to organization decision-makers who are responsible for approving communications. As the situation warrants, you may want to use other personnel, technical experts and outside consultants to bolster your position, but always try to keep the same PR spokesperson as your customary public face.

DEVELOPING A CRISIS COMMUNICATIONS PLAN

After some brainstorming and discussion, you should be able to identify the basic potential problems in your business or organization that might lead to a crisis and possibly balloon into a genuine public relations crisis.

The next step is to determine who would be most negatively affected by the bad news – Customers? Stockholders? Employees? Management? Older people? Younger people? The local community in general? This will help target your crisis PR plan.

Of course, creating a crisis communications plan in-house will save money, compared to hiring an outside PR contractor, but it still will require some time and money to achieve its goals. Your organization should be fully committed to budgeting for both day-to-day public relations and extra expenses in "crisis mode."

It also should be understood that your public relations specialist/spokesperson may need to divert from their other duties to properly function during a crisis.

Management personnel and owners should take the lead and make themselves available to the PR person to answer questions; approve expenditures and communications; and generally lend their support to the effort.

USE YOUR ORGANIZATION'S FACT SHEET AND MEDIA KIT

It's vital to have materials prepared and approved in advance and ready to distribute in order to respond quickly to a public relations crisis. One of the most useful items is your fact sheet, which must be kept up-to-date whenever changes occur in the organization.

A current fact sheet will help reporters gain an accurate overview of your operation and direct them to your PR spokesperson for more information. See Chapter 8 for details on producing fact sheets.

The fact sheet is the centerpiece of your standard media kit, which also should be employed during a public relations crisis. Media kits are covered in Chapter 11.

MAKE SURE EVERYONE KNOWS THEIR ROLE IN A CRISIS

Employees should understand who is in charge of dealing with the press in the organization. Even in normal, *noncrisis* times, every member of your business or organization needs to know that not just anyone should make statements to reporters. This concept is never more important than during a crisis, and cannot be stressed enough.

After your PR effort is well under way and the crisis communications plan is complete, meet with members of your organization to inform them of the plan and what is expected of them.

A brief – preferably single-page – *"Media Communications Plan"* should be produced to guide members of your organization in dealing with the media. It's vital to present the material in such a way that it's clear the policy is not directed at any particular employee: that no one has done anything wrong; and that the rules apply to everyone, not just the lower echelons.

The Media Communications Plan – don't label it a "Crisis Communications Plan" – serves to put people on notice that they should be careful when dealing with the media and that their words – even jokes and casual conversations – may be repeated to harmful effect. By setting out guidelines and consequences for acting outside of the plan, it helps everyone take the crisis communication plan seriously.

WHAT TO TELL YOUR PEOPLE ABOUT THE MEDIA

Most importantly, do not characterize the media as "the enemy." The whole purpose of the crisis communication plan is to prevent misinformation and rumor from damaging the organization. Most of the time, reporters are performing a valuable service for the community by uncovering information and presenting it in an unbiased and timely manner.

Use your organization's "Media Communications Plan" as a jumping-off point to inform members what is expected of them in a PR crisis and generally make them more aware and media-savvy. The crisis PR policy will help everyone deal with the media and when approached by anyone with potentially damaging questions.

RECOGNIZE THAT YOU'RE TALKING TO A REPORTER

Reporters are supposed to identify themselves as such at the beginning of a telephone call, but this isn't always the case. In person, some reporters will begin asking questions without saying who they are and mentioning their employer.

Reporters sometimes try to gain answers from rank-and-file people when they're not getting what they want from higher-ups. To that end, they sometimes neglect to identify themselves as reporters, or even misrepresent themselves. This practice is most common over the telephone.

In the worst cases, reporters may actively misrepresent themselves in an attempt to "go undercover" and trick people into revealing incriminating information. While these methods might be appropriate to entrap mobsters or sexual predators, it's generally frowned upon as an interview technique to be used on ordinary business people and employees.

Unless you personally know the person you're talking to on the telephone, politely ask them to identify themselves: "Can I get your name, who you're with and what you're calling about?"

Despite denials or other claims, there often are clues that it's a reporter trying to surreptitiously pump you for information:

Over the phone: Newsrooms are busy, loud places. Listen for background office sounds – other reporters on calls, telephones ringing or a police scanner. You may notice numerous pauses in the conversation while the reporter is writing. A telltale echo-chamber sound produced by a speaker phone on the other end may indicate the call is being recorded.

In person: If the person takes notes on a small pad or uses a recorder, ask what their intentions are and are they a reporter. In many states, people need your permission to legally record a conversation. A reporter also may be carrying a camera or is with someone who has one that stays in the background and doesn't talk directly to you.

Their demeanor: Is the person asking questions from a prepared list? Do they seem overly aggressive? Are they focusing on what seem to be negative elements of a situation? Are their questions related to a current news story? If so, you're probably dealing with a reporter.

If you're located in a small town or rural area, you may already know the few reporters that cover your community. If you're in a big city, take some time to become familiar with reporters whose "beats" – areas of responsibility – make it likely they would contact organization members

KEEP IT SIMPLE AND STRAIGHTFORWARD

The best way to deal with reporters is to let someone else do it. If your company or organization authorizes someone to talk to the media, they can inadvertently get into trouble if they choose to display their amusing character and sparkling wit.

Don't try to be funny or sarcastic – even if the reporter gets your meaning, a literal transcript of your words in a story probably won't convey your intentions correctly to readers. Don't speculate, repeat rumors or say anything you're not 100 percent sure about. Groundless statements are exactly counterproductive to what you're trying to achieve with a crisis communication plan.

Similarly, refrain whenever possible from voicing your personal opinion. Such statements are easily taken as fact by third parties and are a prime breeding ground for damaging rumors. Even rumors or opinions voiced by you to a co-worker, friend or family member may be repeated to a reporter and published or broadcast.

Be careful. If you make a mistake and say something that isn't true or image-enhancing, it may be impossible to take it back. Saying as little as possible, while still handling legitimate concerns from the public, is a good habit. Don't let an interview wander. Keep it short and simple.

While the reporter is not your *enemy*, they also are not your *friend* or *confidante*. They will jump on anything you say that's "newsy" and use it. Any conversation you have with a reporter can used, even if it seems not part of the actual interview itself.

Even "off the record" statements can open the door to a damaging line of inquiry for a reporter after the interview with you is over.

SAMPLE MEDIA COMMUNICATIONS PLAN

On the following page is an example of a media communications plan that would be distributed to employees, organization members and anyone privy to details of your operation. Printed plans like this always should contain a statement up front that recognizes and respects the role of the media in serving the public, because a copy may fall into a reporter's hands.

The plan also should make it clear the organization is serious about controlling unauthorized media contact and sets forth possible disciplinary action. The plan should be explained orally, questions answered, and then should be signed by each party, dated and filed.

Media Communications Plan

Overview

As an organization whose employees interact with the public and may be questioned by print and broadcast media representatives, such as reporters, it is important that only accurate and truthful information reaches the community at large about the activities and policies of **Pete's Golf Cars, Inc.**, hereafter referred to as "company."

To that end, this plan has been developed to help protect company employees and the public they serve from damaging rumors and speculation arising from unauthorized statements and misinformation. Adherence to this plan will help reduce the risk of legal liability to all concerned caused by dissemination of factual errors or personal opinions.

The company recognizes the legitimate need for the public to be informed about its activities and policies, and the important role of print and broadcast media to provide that information, and have implemented this Plan to assist that process.

Implementation

To deal with media contact, company management has designated a public relations representative, who should be the sole and key contact for all inquiries by the media.

Unless specifically authorized by company management, employees should not act as spokespersons for the company and should refer all media inquiries to the public relations representative.

Company management may authorize or designate employees, contractors, attorneys or other persons to speak on behalf of the company.

In responding to questions and concerns from the general public, company employees should refrain from speculation and opinion and present only factual information directly related to the inquiry.

Policy

All company employees shall be provided a copy of this Media Communications Plan and are expected to abide by its requirements.

Failure to comply with this plan and policy may result in review and disciplinary action by company management.

This policy does not apply to inquiries from law enforcement or other authorized government agents, in which case employees are advised to consult their manager.

I have read and understand this policy:

_____   _____
Signature   Date

RUMOR CONTROL

People love gossip and rumors: They're usually much more interesting and juicy than the truth. The rumor mill and local grapevine are big components in the flow of information, but not necessarily *correct* information.

Thanks to the Internet – the malicious rumormonger's biggest asset – rumors are more prolific and damaging than ever before. If you endure a rumor-based PR crisis, chances are good it began as an Internet posting. Blogs, forums and e-mails spread misinformation fast – and on the Web, rumors never die, but live on forever, easily discovered by search engines to wreak new havoc years after they first circulated.

What can you do, public relations-wise, if a rumor is finding an audience, proliferating and damaging your operation?

To begin with, determine the damage potential of the rumor and disregard it if possible, because most countermeasures have the unfortunate short-term effect of actually helping to spread the rumor and lending some legitimacy to it.

If the rumor is persistent and a real threat, supply information to the media directly addressing and countering the rumor. It often helps to point out the potential damage to the community at large from the rumor – unemployment, ridicule, bad public image, demoralization, decreased tourism, etc. Personally contact local leaders to counter the rumor and enlist their help to do the same.

It's not unknown for companies to combat rumors by spreading *counter-rumors* via the Internet or with a word-of-mouth operation. Again, this type of crafty countermeasure can backfire by lengthening the life of the original rumor and lending it credence it doesn't deserve.

CRISIS AFTERMATH

When it's all over and normalcy is restored, pose the questions, "Why did this crisis happen? Can it happen again? What has been done to prevent it from happening again? Was our crisis communication plan effective?"

Few learning opportunities in public relations are as valuable as looking back over a crisis and trying to figure out what happened. Every system, safeguard and person in your communications setup will have been tested under fire. Your organization may have found previously hidden problems – as well as untapped strengths and resources.

Hopefully, you'll have the time and commitment to your PR effort to examine it and make changes. Remember, the crisis may be past – or it may have been just the first wave in a series of setbacks and challenges.

CRISIS MANAGEMENT TIPS

In general, good public relations methods and ethics are never more valuable than when engaged in a PR crisis. Here's a short list of useful tips and techniques:

- With long- or short-term problems, the challenge is to maintain credibility. If you attempt a cover-up, you're asking for trouble.

- Don't give the unwanted job of putting-off the media to the receptionist.

- The telephone is your friend. Always try to answer it. Don't hide behind an answering machine.

- The media should be given only established facts, not guesses. Better to say, "The cause still is undetermined," or, "I don't know, but I'll try to find out."

- Unfavorable news should not be concealed.

- A positive spin should be attempted whenever possible.

- Make a special effort to give favorable facts to the media, such as calling attention to prompt actions that minimized damage, injuries or financial loss.

- The media should be notified of important information immediately, and reporters sent to cover a situation should not be viewed as intruders.

- Often, a crisis can be avoided with good, honest and timely information.

- Speculate about nothing.

- Openness may be a problem in legal matters afterward, but it does foster good public opinion.

- Keep a level head. Don't let your emotional state produce pronounced attitudes of anger, depression, surprise or even exuberance. The person who faces the media must project a calm and professional demeanor.

- Don't spar with reporters.

- Don't view the media as an enemy or a threat. If you disengage from them, they will get the story from less-reliable, less-friendly sources.

- Inform internally first. Your people are the first that need to know what's going on.

- Avoid the temptation to be witty or sarcastic.

- "Stonewalling" is the worst response to press queries. It merely alerts reporters that something is brewing and they'll turn to other sources of information.

- Organize materials in advance and have them ready to distribute, focused around your current, up-to-date fact sheet.

- Keep your answers plain and short. Reporters are interested in simple, single-issue explanations that are easy to write and that the readers can grasp quickly.

- Do not simply refuse to answer a difficult question. Give your reason.

- Think of the media as a valuable resource to tell your side of the story and channel positive news.

- Remember that reporters are not your friends, but neither are they your enemies.

- Real, verifiable information squelches rumors.

- Highlighting only management people and their positive, mitigating role in a crisis can make the organization appear top-heavy and stratified. Make an effort to spread the credit vertically throughout the organization.

- Stress previous measures taken to try to avert the present crisis and how it could have been much worse if not for your diligence.

- Think about who is affected most by the crisis, and focus the tone and direction of your response toward that audience.

- If you foresee the crisis approaching, consider a "preemptive strike" by issuing a news release with your positive perspective before the storm breaks.

- Play up efforts to reduce the negative impact of your crisis on others, such as customers, children or the elderly.

- Estimate the extra expense a crisis might entail, and budget accordingly.

- Foster a friendly, open, honest, ongoing relationship with the media during noncrisis times. This goodwill will serve you well when you're in trouble.

- Pick your PR spokesperson based on not only on their communications skills, but their personality, voice and appearance. They will be the face of your business or organization in a crisis.

YOU'RE A JOURNALIST NOW

When you publish or broadcast something, you're subject to the same protections – and restrictions – that have been established for journalists. Because of their power to influence people and the potential to misuse or abuse that power, journalists have a special place in society and the law.

For that reason, they're often called the "fourth estate," a distinct class apart from the rest of their fellow citizens.

KNOW THE LAW

In the United States, laws concerning journalists and the media ultimately stem from a common source, the First Amendment to the U.S. Constitution, in the Bill of Rights:

> *Congress shall make no law respecting an establishment of religion, or prohibiting the free exercise thereof; or abridging the freedom of speech, or of the press; or the right of the people peaceably to assemble, and to petition the Government for a redress of grievances.*

While First Amendment rights provide a blanket of protection and allow a wide latitude of activities for American journalists, another body of regulations and case law has developed over the years, based on the concepts of libel and the right of privacy.

Libel and privacy case law is one of several restraints on press freedom. Press control already exists by means of censorship and harsh penalties, such as:

- Reporters may not commit crimes to get a story, such as cooperating with gangsters or participating in a burglary.
- Obscenity laws, which are more and more dependent on "local standards."
- Self-regulation within the industry, such as "broadcast standards."
- Government regulation – antitrust laws, anti-wiretapping laws, etc.
- Licensing – radio/TV station licenses, press credentials.
- "Clear and Present Danger" – Federal laws that address threats to society in general.

LIBEL

A libel is a published or broadcast statement that unjustifiably exposes someone to ridicule or contempt, harming them in some way. Libel and slander are basically the same thing, except slander is spoken, while a libelous statement must be published in some way – newspapers, magazines, publicly displayed posters, books, radio, television, an Internet Web site and the like.

Libel is nearly always a civil action – not a crime – brought against a reporter, an author or a publisher by an individual plaintiff. Groups cannot sue for libel. "Criminal libel" exists as a legal concept, but is tied to other crimes. An example would be inciting a riot against a business by publishing false accusations about it.

THE 'ELEMENTS OF LIBEL'

There are five elements of libel, *all* of which must be proven by the plaintiff to win a court case. If one is missing, no libel occurred. To be considered libelous, a statement must:

1. **DEFAME** – Smear or stigmatize in some way.

2. **IDENTIFY** – By name, appearance, circumstance, group affiliation, association with a named companion, etc. People who read or see the statement must be able to identify the person, even if that person was not actually named.

3. **BE PUBLISHED** – That is, communicated to a third party.

4. **BE FALSE** – Demonstratively or provably untrue.

5. **HARM** – This usually means money – a financial loss, but also can mean pain and suffering, loss of reputation, mental anguish. Harm must be directly tied to the alleged libel and the writer or media organization that created it.

WHAT IS A 'DEFAMATORY STATEMENT?'

Remember, a defamatory statement that's *true* is not libelous. There are as many possible ways to defame someone as there are stars in the night sky, but a few methods stand out:

- Accuse of a crime.
- Accuse business or occupational incompetence, malpractice or dishonesty.
- Accuse of having a loathsome disease.
- Question chastity – usually of a woman.
- Allege a sexual preference.
- Defame by "outside circumstances" – Accomplished with statements such as "seen with mobsters" or "pulled over during a DUI sweep."

GROUP DEFAMATION

Because libel requires an *individual* plaintiff, groups cannot sue for libel. However, an individual may allege libel if they are linked in a defamatory way to the actions or beliefs of a group, such as neo-Nazis or terrorists.

There is no libel, however, if a group is so large that a reasonable person would not suspect that an individual is guilty of an act attributed to the group. For example, a Muslim man could not sue a newspaper for libel on the grounds it ran a story on an Islamic militant bomb plot, and the man suffered accordingly by loss of reputation in the community.

THE DEFENSES OF LIBEL

There are 10 basic defenses of libel. Some are "absolute defenses," meaning they are facts or arguments that, if proven, will end litigation in favor of the defendant. Journalists employ them all the time, and they certainly apply to public relations work.

1. Statute of Limitations
This is one year in most states. It's reasonable to assume that an offended individual will have become aware of a potential libel and take legal action within that time.

2. Privilege of Reporting
Called "the journalist's 'bread and butter defense.'" Anything said or done during an official public proceeding can be repeated in a news publication. This includes public meetings, court proceedings, elections and governmental functions. No "truth check" is needed on statements made during an official proceeding as long as the reporting is accurate.

3. New York Times vs. Sullivan ruling (*aka* "The Sullivan Rule")
Public figures have almost no protection from libel, but stories about public figures must concern their public life and not solely the private doings. Nothing in such stories can be a knowing lie or reckless disregard for the truth – otherwise known as "malice." Public figures include politicians, officials, clergy and persons involved in events of public or general interest.

This defense stems from a 1964 U.S. Supreme Court case, which determined that a public official cannot collect damages unless they can prove "actual malice," defined as, "Knowledge that it (the publication) was false, or with reckless disregard of whether it was false or not."

Two years later, in 1966, the Supreme Court expanded the Sullivan ruling to include "public figures" as well as public officials. In 1971, it was expanded to include persons involved in an event of public or general interest, which meant *many* types of public figures or "celebrities," such as musicians, professional athletes, movie stars, etc.

4. Truth

This is "The Big One" in libel defenses – an absolute defense. It means *provably* true in court, so be prepared to back up a provocative statement. And remember, a true statement still can constitute an invasion of privacy.

5. Fair Comment and Criticism

Professional and amateur writers alike are free to present opinions – as long as those opinions are clearly subjective and do not pose as factual "hard news." Opinion is not libel, but can be defamatory.

Anyone who offers a service to the public for pay or who performs for pay or no pay is open to subjective criticism – actors, musicians, restaurateurs, street mimes, auto mechanics, caterers, dog groomers. Often, business owners that get a bad review in a publication try to sue for libel, but reviews and ratings are protected under the fair comment and criticism principle.

6. Consent

In this absolute defense, the plaintiff clearly gave their permission to publish the allegedly libelous information. This consent can be friendly and consensual, or could be in the form of an angry challenge – "Go ahead and print that and see what happens!" It's important to secure the consent in a format that will hold up in court, such as a signed agreement or legally recorded conversation.

7. Right of Reply

This is a sort of verbal self-defense, alleging that the libel occurred in the "heat of exchange," such as an argumentative debate. You might think it applies mainly to verbal libel – slander – but such statements can be broadcast, and thus, *published*.

In another type of reply defense, the libeled party is presented with an opportunity to respond. Whether they reply or not is not important, as long as the offer was made in good faith to publish the reply in the same manner as the original libel. Note: A published response should not exceed the provocation of the piece that prompted it.

8. Accord and Satisfaction

This means the parties involved reached an agreement to resolve the libel case. It usually means money is paid, but could involve an apology or other arrangement.

9. Dissemination within a "community of interest"

Potentially libelous information can be found in medical and scientific journals and other professional or academic media. This is not usually considered "publication" for the purposes of libel.

10. Satire

Published humor that ridicules someone is allowed, but there are rules. Such pieces must be clearly labeled "satire" – however small – and should not be mixed with real news stories.

Satire should only be used on public figures and performers, not the average person. The principle is that for satire to be defensible, the object of the satire should have a large number of people already familiar with them and be able to recognize the story as satire.

MORE ABOUT PRIVILEGE OF REPORTING

Libel or invasion of privacy torts cannot be filed when stories or photographs stem from circumstances of privilege of reporting – that is, covering the functions of government, including the courts.

Can you *repeat* a libel in reporting about it? Yes, this falls under privilege of reporting. However, many states do not recognize privilege when the case is filed, only during the actual court proceedings – so a legal sword could be hanging over your head for months.

Keep in mind **four rules** on privilege of reporting:

1. **Be Fair.**
2. **Be Accurate.**
3. **Name the forum – What, when and where was the proceeding?**
4. **Be certain it's an *official and public* proceeding.**

PARTIAL LIBEL DEFENSES

A successful partial defense can decrease damage awards for a defendant found guilty of libel. There are four basic types

1. **Corrections Statute** – Running a speedy correction might reduce general damages.

2. **General reputation of a person** – A case can be won on this point, but a plaintiff's generally bad reputation will more likely reduce general damages.

3. **Rumor** – A last-ditch defense. Usually not very successful.

4. **Innocent construction rule** – Can the alleged libel be interpreted in a more innocent, nondefamatory way? If so, the innocent construction will be assumed by the law.

CORRECTIONS

Corrections should be printed or broadcast quickly. Most states have a corrections statute, which outlines the procedure necessary by both plaintiff and publisher. It usually entails the plaintiff sending written notice to the media after knowledge of the publication or broadcast, a time limit for the media to issue a correction, as well as other special considerations, such as applicability in elections and allowable damages.

Publishing and distributing corrections will not get you off the hook entirely if you have libeled someone, but in certain cases it can eliminate general damages. Corrections statutes do not necessarily apply to magazines, but always to newspapers.

The corrections statutes of the various states are similar, but differ in the details. Check out your state's law online to understand. In some states, for example, here's how it's supposed to work:

1. The plaintiff must send written notice – a "demand letter" – within 20 days after actual knowledge of publication or broadcast.

2. Within three weeks after service of the demand letter, a correction must be published or broadcast in substantially as conspicuous a manner as the claimed libel.

3. Punitive damages can be awarded only if actual malice is proven.

4. The correction statute does not apply to any publication or broadcast within 30 days of an election if it is designed to influence the results of that election.

THE RIGHT OF PRIVACY

Invasion of privacy is the publicizing of information about a person without legitimate and legal purpose. Photographs make up most these cases – see the "Legal Considerations in PR Photography" section of Chapter 10 – Photographs – but the concepts equally apply to printed and broadcast text and statements.

Violation of someone's privacy rights is a civil offense – a "tort" – and not a crime. It is a uniquely American legal creation and did not exist as a legal principle before 1890. Since then, the idea of the "right to be left alone" has grown over the years, and is susceptible to broad interpretation in the courts.

Right to privacy legal questions arose after newspapers widely adopted hand-held plate and sheet film cameras and could easily and quickly reproduce photographs on the printed page via a perfected halftone process.

In 1890, two Boston lawyers wrote in the Harvard Law Review:

> *"The press is overstepping in every direction the obvious bounds of propriety and decency."*

In the 1928 Olmstead vs. United States decision, Supreme Court Associate Justice Louis Brandeis wrote a dissenting opinion that has been cited countless times in invasion of privacy cases:

> *"The makers of our Constitution undertook to secure conditions favorable to the pursuit of happiness. They recognized the significance of man's spiritual nature, of his feelings and his intellect. They knew that only a part of the pain, pleasure and satisfactions of life are to be found in material things. They sought to protect Americans in their beliefs, their thoughts, their emotions and their sensations. They conferred, as against the government, the right to be let alone – the most comprehensive or rights and the right most valued by civilized men."*

Olmstead, who had been convicted of illegal alcohol peddling based partly on evidence obtained via telephone wiretaps, lost his appeal before the Supreme Court 5 to 4, but was later pardoned by the President.

INVASION OF PRIVACY'S FOUR BASIC LEGAL AND ETHICAL QUESTIONS:

- Was the information acquired legally?

- Was there trespassing on private property?

- Did the alleged invasion of privacy occur in the course of covering a legitimate news story? Was the story "newsworthy" and "timely?"

- Is information about the plaintiff, story or photo, being used to unjustly enrich the writer, photographer or publication? That is, *without consent*.

FOUR MAJOR TYPES OF INVASION OF PRIVACY SUITS:

1. **Intrusion.** Upon a person's physical or mental solitude. Two prime areas of concern are home and hospital.

2. **Private Facts.** That is, information acquired by trespassing on private property, poking into nonpublic records, questioning minors and other sources that the law recognizes as private and protected.

3. **False Light.** Fictionalization – mixing facts and fiction. Akin to libel.

4. **Appropriation.** Is information about the plaintiff – story or image – being used to unjustly enrich the writer, photographer or publication? That is, without consent. If you're going to use an identifiable person for advertising or "for purposes of trade," which includes public relations work, then written consent is the best defense against an invasion of privacy suit.

NEWSWORTHINESS

If published information or photograph is more than a day or two old, or does not relate to a current, breaking news story, its "newsworthiness" is questionable and may expose its creators to an invasion of privacy suit. For example:

A child was injured in an auto accident in Alabama. A newspaper took a picture of the scene before the child was removed and ran it. That was "spot news," and was an acceptable and legal use of the image. Twenty months later, a magazine used the picture to illustrate an article on auto safety. The magazine was sued for invasion of privacy and lost the case - The court ruled that 20 months after the accident, the child was no longer "in the news."

BASIC DEFENSES FOR INVASION OF PRIVACY

For the journalist and public relations writer or photographer, two clear paths are open to defend themselves when charged with invasion of someone's privacy.

1. That the person or event is newsworthy or of "immediate interest." The weakness of this defense is that it is open to wide interpretation.

2. Consent, particularly if the information is used for advertising or "purposes of trade." Such consent ideally should be in writing, dated and witnessed to avoid legal challenge.

WHO GETS SUED FOR LIBEL OR INVASION OF PRIVACY?

The author? The photographer? The editor? The publication? The source of the alleged libel? In our modern litigious society, *anyone* even remotely linkable to a civil suit can find themselves pulled into the case as a defendant. The usual answer to this question is the party with the "deepest pockets."

DAMAGES

Successful plaintiffs in libel cases are compensated by receiving damages, usually in the form of money. There are three types of damages:

1. **Special** – These are losses linked to the libel that can be proven, itemized and receipts produced. Election losses usually are not considered elements of damage.

2. **General** – Considerations for more ephemeral kinds of harm, such as loss of reputation, pain and suffering, emotional duress. Dollar-wise, most damages awarded in libel cases are general.

3. **Punitive** – Damages above and beyond special and general losses, awarded to make an example of a losing defendant. A plaintiff must prove actual malice – reckless disregard for the truth – to gain a chance at punitive damages.

AVOIDING LIBEL AND INVASION OF PRIVACY PROBLEMS

Just because a libel or privacy tort is filed, or damages are demanded with or without formal legal action, doesn't mean the case has a reasonable basis and any chance at all of success, but it still will suck up lots of time and money for the unfortunate defendant.

Far better to avoid the obvious pitfalls and steer wide of potential problems by recognizing danger signals early and adopting smart operating procedure. Here are some tips:

- Clear the story's contents with those concerned, or obtain written permission to use their information, if possible.

- Record telephone and face-to-face interviews whenever you can. Begin a recording with a description of what is going on, the date, who you are interviewing, etc. Digital voice recorders do a better job than tape models, and the voice files are easy to archive on your computer. Keep digital voice files or tapes for at least a year. Don't get lazy and let recorders take the place of written notes – do both. If someone objects to the presence of a recorder, be on the alert for lies, innuendo and statements they intend to deny later. Tell them the recording is for their protection.

- Check your state's consent" laws concerning recording conversations legally. "One-party consent" means just one party to the chat must know it's being taped – that of course would be the person doing the taping. "Two party" means the party being recorded must be informed for the recording to be of any legal use later.

- Watch out for errors of fact, especially when they involve identification of people.

- Avoid impoverished publications that are likely to be without competent editing, fact-checking, libel insurance or a lawyer on retainer.

- Know the elements of libel. Read up, be aware of precedent.

- Choose carefully who you include in an article.

- Be careful of characterizing a group – it may be a very small group and its members may be subject to identification and ridicule.

- The dead cannot be libeled, although heirs keep trying to sue. Make sure that a potentially libelous article about a dead person does not cast aspersions on the living.

- Inspect your text and photos meticulously. Look at them with a "dirty mind;" with the mind of a religious fanatic; with the mind of a litigious troublemaker.

- Despite the "Innocent Construction rule," consider – Is there *any way* that *anyone* could take offense or interpret the material in a defamatory way?

- Homes are the place of greatest privacy rights.

PROTECTIONS FOR REPORTERS AND PHOTOGRAPHERS

In the course of doing PR work, you function, in fact, as a journalist, and in addition to the responsibilities and restraints imposed on the media, you benefit from some of the protections established to keep the press working in a free and practical manner.

The concept of "privilege of reporting" allows reporters to effectively cover government functions, such as courts and legislatures, while "shield" laws give them the same basic protection as doctors and lawyers to information sources, but with limitations.

SHIELD LAWS

The concept is that certain parties have legal exemption from testifying, revealing sources or surrendering notes or negatives because of a *broad social reason*.

Exemptions include husbands and wives, attorneys and clients, doctors and patients, the Fifth Amendment guard against self-incrimination, clerical privilege and reporter-informant confidentiality – also known as "shield laws."

Contrary to widespread public belief, there is no *federal* reporter shield law. Reporters must still testify before grand juries and their private notes can subpoenaed.

If a state's shield law statute contains wording such as "overriding public necessity, "national defense" or "critical to a fair trial," then it is useless to the media.

Such exceptions make the law essentially powerless to protect journalists. Even in states where a reporter cannot be compelled by any agency to disclose sources, judges find ways to impose penalties – including jail time – for reporters who don't cooperate.

SHIELD LAW INCURSIONS BY GOVERNMENT

Government attorneys have been busy for decades, chipping away at the laws that legislators create to protect journalists, and in the process creating a sometimes-contradictory body of case law.

As it stands, a person must be a working reporter to use a state's shield law. Although the definition of "working reporter" remains open to interpretation and the discretion of a judge. Reporters also must *immediately* report or disclose information to the police if witness to or aware of a crime, which effectively strikes down reporter-informant protections.

Based on the Sixth Amendment's guarantee of rights to a "speedy and public trial" and access to witnesses both for and against the accused, if a reporter's knowledge is critical to someone getting a fair trial, they must testify and be cooperative – which can include revealing sources.

There is no "First Amendment Shield." Reporters must testify before federal bodies like other citizens. A California court held that the government must show that it has exhausted other sources of information, and detail that search, to obtain a reporter's notes or testimony, but that ruling was overturned by the U.S. Supreme Court.

Defenses can be struck and a default judgment entered if a reporter is not "cooperative" during deposition. Finally, a client can sue his lawyer if the lawyer reveals confidential information, but there is no similar protection for a reporter's informant.

LICENSING OF JOURNALISTS AND PRESS CREDENTIALS

Every few years, the idea of licensing reporters is resurrected by some Washington politician who thinks they've been unfairly treated by the media. These proposals get shot down with a lot of bombastic rhetoric by other politicians and in newspaper editorials, but the fact is there has been *de facto* licensing of journalists for more than a hundred years.

The First Amendment of the U.S. Constitution guarantees freedom of speech and the press, but does not define what "the press" actually is. At the time the Constitution was written, newspapers as we understand them today did not exist and media-related laws and precedent were nearly non-existent.

Just as freedom of speech is not narrowly interpreted to mean it protects only paid, professional *orators*, it can be reasonably assumed that freedom of the press likely should extend to all levels of the published media, from the fringe-kook eccentric who cranks out a single mimeograph page screed every 50 years to Internet bloggers to billionaire media tycoons. Some people claim if you publish, you're a member of the press, according to the U.S. Constitution.

Instead, we have a system where journalists effectively are licensed on the local level by some police sergeant. Law enforcement issues "press credentials" with the cooperation of the major media outlets - radio, television, newspapers, magazines. A letter from the publisher and a phone call are all that's needed to be a government-recognized journalist.

Unconstitutional? Probably, but newspapers and TV stations go along with this because it helps give them exclusivity to the news: Only their reporters and photographers can get close to the newsmakers, go backstage and cross checkpoints.

And finally, police and government officials are usually wary of and brusque toward journalists, including freelancers and public relations types with a notepad, voice recorder or camera. They do not want their actions recorded, and will sometimes go to surprising lengths to avoid and bully reporters or anyone who looks and acts like one.

The omnipresent camcorder in the hands of nearly everyone everywhere is changing the situation dramatically, but the "us versus them" mindset is alive and well in most police departments. In short, no matter how innocent and legal your activity, be prepared for a hassle when from law enforcement. It does no good to complain or resist – just live with it.

COPYRIGHTS

Bear in mind that material created for public relations purposes succeeds best when it is copied, published and viewed by the largest possible audience. To this end, affixing a copyright notice on any PR submittal would be counterproductive.

However, for whatever reason, you may wish to ensure copyright protection on something created in the course of public relations work.

In this age of easily duplicated or pirated intellectual property, copyrights help protect the original works of authors, composers, programmers, artists and the like against illegal copies and plagiarism, and allow creators of such works control and profit.

Copyright is a legal concept, usually enforced by civil actions. In the United States, the Copyright Clause of the Constitution enabled copyright law to be developed. In 1989, the United States signed onto the Berne Convention, which streamlines copyright protection by eliminating the need for formal registration of works.

Now, as soon as a work is "fixed" – that is, written or recorded on some physical medium – including computer hard drives – its creator is entitled to full copyright protection. No actual copyright notice is needed and no registration with the national government is required.

Although copyright notices are now optional, they may confer enhanced infringement protection to authors. The notice consists of the word "copyright" or the copyright symbol, followed by the date – usually the current year – and your name. For example,

©**2011 Michael R. Gearlds**

Forget about sending your works to yourself in a sealed envelope via certified mail to establish copyright. This unnecessary practice is a kind of "urban legend" and is not recognized by the courts.

Copyright legal concepts are pretty straightforward and understandable. Several excellent guides to copyright law are available online for free.

TRADEMARKS AND PATENTS

There are fundamental differences between a copyright and a trademark: Copyrights protect all sorts of intellectual property, while trademarks govern the protected use of words, phrases, symbols and designs that distinguish the products or services of one party from those of others. Examples would be a company's logo or the distinctive sign in front of all chain restaurants. Oftentimes a company will trademark catch phrases used in televised ads, like, "Have it your way," or "The heartbeat of America."

While are the laws and regulations governing copyrights are somewhat casual and compliance-friendly, trademarks usually must be registered to be enforceable.

If you use an unregistered trademark only within your own state – maybe a local restaurant or hardware store – you can put a "TM" or "SM" next to your logo and the like in advertisements and signage, standing for "trademark" or "service mark," respectively. This is called "common-law" protection.

However, if you do business in more than one state, including business on the Internet, you should register your trademark with the U.S. Patent and Trademark Office. After completing an application and paying fees, your trademark is examined to determine if it is unique and suitable for trademark protection. Then it is published for 30 days in an official federal book for public review and potential opposition.

If all goes well and no one objects to your trademark, you will receive a "Certificate of Registration" or "Notice of Allowance," depending on the type of application you submitted. You then must then submit a "Statement of Use," which, when filed by the Patent Office, entitles you to use the ® trademark symbol next to your protected items.

The trademark-registering process is sufficiently complicated to probably warrant the services of an attorney or legal-services company that specializes in such things.

As far as patents go, the application process is much more involved and costly and beyond the concern of public relations. However, if you do hold a patent of any kind and it is relevant to your PR effort, it is important to feature it in news releases and other public relations materials.

WORK FOR HIRE

A writer or photographer usually is the sole owner of a copyright, but in cases where they are hired – and *paid* – to create the intellectual property for an employer, customer or client, most courts probably would say the employer, customer or client is entitled to the copyright. This is called "work for hire."

If a creator can show they were *never paid* by a client for the work for hire, they probably can lay claim to the copyright.

BE PREPARED TO "LAWYER-UP"

The legal concepts outlined in this chapter are intended to help keep you out of trouble by trying to avoid problems *before* you publish something. To this end, college journalism curriculums always include courses on legal aspects of the profession.

But if someday you find yourself on the receiving end of a lawsuit stemming from your writing, photography or other public relations-related activity, no amount of quoting the

First Amendment or citing **DO YOUR OWN PUBLIC RELATIONS!** will spare you the time and expense of engaging the services of a competent lawyer.

"A person who acts as their own attorney has a fool for a client," goes the old adage, and you will definitely need a specialist who knows the workings of the legal system and how to mount a vigorous defense.

You will, however, by reading this book be armed with a fundamental grasp of the law as it pertains to journalism in general and public relations in particular. This should help you work with your attorney in the unfortunate event that you need one.

Chapter 15: Legal Considerations

CHAPTER 16
<u>MEASURING RESULTS</u>

WAS YOUR PR EFFORT EFFECTIVE?

Your public relations undertaking may have resulted in print media or television coverage, but how can you tell if it worked? Has the publicity made people more aware of and more favorably inclined toward you? How have you benefited?

Before beginning a campaign, public relations agencies often will commission a survey of public opinion concerning their client. That survey will guide them in identifying what issues need to be addressed and what audiences, media and methods on which to focus.

Surveys at mid-campaign can point out what changes might be needed to the public relations effort, and a final survey at the end will give some indication of how well it all worked.

Hiring an outside consultant to do a public opinion survey is expensive, and such surveying is at best an imprecise science, subject to various errors. The design of the survey itself may have flaws, such as leading or ambiguous questions, that make it virtually useless.

The good news is there are ways for you to gauge the effectiveness of your public relations work, but don't expect a high degree of precision – even professionals can't promise that.

DETERMINING EFFECTIVE PUBLIC RELATIONS

Placement in newspapers and magazines
Did your news release result in a published story, either plucked whole from your release or based on it? Did it generate multiple placements? Did people see it and let you know?

Radio/Television air time
Did your release generate some broadcast time? Do people remember the story?

Sales/traffic volumes
Wait a week or so after your news release resulted in a published or broadcast story and check your receipts, number of walk-ins, inquiry calls and other indicators of interest. Compare them to similar statistics you gathered immediately before the placement. Was there a measurable improvement? Be careful that your perceptions are not skewed by your own advertising, seasonal demands or other external factors.

Talk to your customers and clients
Did these people read, listen to or watch the story your news release generated? What did they think? Are people mentioning the story without being prompted? Beware of flattery – you may have to dig a little to get an honest opinion.

Did your own employees read it?

Was the media material resulting from your news release interesting enough for your own people to notice and stick with to the end? Too many organizations with regular newsletters find out to their dismay that their own employees don't bother to read them – a pretty good sign the material within is not newsworthy, interesting, useful or enjoyable. A valuable lesson here is that most newsletters are not effective public relations or educational tools and are not worth the time and money spent to produce them

Track media coverage

Now that you're doing in-house public relations, you should start a three-ring binder, called a "clipping book," containing your news releases and other distributed PR material, along with copies of published newspaper and magazine stories about your organization.

Your clipping book should be arranged chronologically, with the newest items on top. Group news releases just beneath any media coverage they may have generated. Everything should be clearly labeled with the date and publication at the upper right of the page.

Be sure to make photocopies of the newspaper stories and use those photocopies, not the originals, in the clip book, because newsprint paper deteriorates quickly. Photocopies stay white and crisp virtually forever. CDs of radio sound files and DVDs of television coverage also deserve a place in your clipping book. This means you'll have to learn some basic skills covering recording, converting and archiving sound and video files.

Avoid punching flimsy holes for the binder rings. Instead, put everything in clear vinyl sleeves. At most office supply stores you'll be able to find sleeves to hold not only standard letter-size sheets, but also the CDs and DVDs.

If at all possible, scan published stories and store the images on CD, because even the most durable hard copies are subject to all kinds of damage from moisture, light, insects, fire, etc. With good scans of your clippings, you'll be able to do quality prints of them, reduce or enlarge the images as needed, and e-mail the files.

Public relations agencies often use third-party media-reporting services to track placements, including broadcast media, and supply copies to them. The PR firm, in turn, supplies the copies to the client at a stiff markup – Handy, but expensive. You can do almost as well by keeping a close eye on the media yourself when expecting some coverage.

DON'T ATTEMPT A PUBLIC OPINION SURVEY OF YOUR OWN

Public opinion surveys are expensive to conduct and usually are done by companies that specialize solely in such work. These companies have the experience and personnel – database specialists, statisticians, interviewers, cubicle-bound telephone staff – to push out surveys quickly and as accurately as possible. Again – handy, but expensive.

There's lots of legwork involved, nearly always by telephone, but also by mail, Internet and "on the street" interviews. Those people you see in big shopping malls, with the clipboards and an eye for certain special subjects to approach in the crowd, are marketing and public-opinion surveyors. Is this really how you want to spend your public relations time and money?

Finally, even professionally done opinion surveys are not very reliable, with a host of things that can go wrong and make the whole effort a dubious undertaking.

KEEP YOUR PUBLIC OPINION RESEARCH LOW-KEY

There are lots of good reasons why it's a bad idea to do your own surveys, but that doesn't mean you can't try to get a handle on the issues you should address. What kind of survey can you do?

For starters, survey your customers. This makes for a very focused population sample – one that you really care about. Friends and family members you can trust to give you honest answers and not flattery also are prime private survey fodder.

Don't try to question hundreds of people. You probably will gain valuable insight into the tenor of public opinion with just a couple dozen contacts.

Restrict your survey to a few simple written questions – no more than six queries – and keep the whole thing short, to two or three minutes, tops. Don't stray from your written questions, keep idle conversation to a minimum.

Follow Yes/No questions with questions seeking detail or clarification, for example: "Do you have a positive or negative impression of XYZ Corp?" "What was the deciding factor in forming your impression?" "Do you remember any published or broadcast stories involving XYZ Corp in the past six months?" "What were they?"

If there's an obvious public relations problem with your organization that's a concern to you, such as recent negative publicity, use that concern as the basis for your survey, but don't *lead* with it. Bury any queries about bad press or nasty rumors midway through your brief list of questions.

Perform the survey in person, not on the telephone. Telemarketers have pretty much turned the entire population of the world against being bothered in their own homes by telephone calls from businesses.

Don't offer incentives to survey respondents, like cash, coupons or small gifts. This will lessen the reliability of their answers and skew your survey population toward people who trade their vaulable time for trinkets.

YOU NEED A BASELINE TO ANALYZE YOUR SURVEY

Just like PR pros would do, do a simple survey *before* your public relations effort, and then resurvey the same group – not necessarily the exact same people, but persons representing the same *type* of respondents, such as walk-in customers – *after* any media attention has occurred.

For the "after" survey, be sure to use the same questions in the same order that were used in the "before" survey.

The "before" survey responses are now your "baseline" to try to measure trends in public opinion. Compare the responses between the two surveys and you'll have some idea of how well your PR succeeded.

Just be aware at all times that determining public opinion via surveys is an inexact science at best, and is subject to so many variables that it's potentially worthless.

CREATE A GOOD PLACE TO WORK

Whether you do your public relations writing at work or at home, it's essential to have reference resources ready at hand. Anything you use to write your PR materials should be kept within arm's reach. At a *minimum*, consider these four items:

- **The Associated Press Stylebook**
- **Webster's New World College Dictionary**
- **Your own local style sheet**
- **Your word processor's custom dictionary that's used for spell-checking, updated with the entries from your local style sheet**

By now, you know the latest edition of the AP Stylebook will be your constant companion as you write materials for the media. The "Webster's New World College Dictionary" also is a must-have. It's the dictionary used by the Associated Press.

Interestingly, "Webster's" is not a copyrighted term, and can be found on all sorts of dictionaries produced by various publishers. Get the one from Wiley Publishing, Inc.

And, believe it or not – English dictionaries *are not all the same* and can vary on spelling, meaning and acceptance of many words.

YOUR OWN STYLE SHEET?

Most newspapers develop their own style sheets, which can be quite extensive. Think of them as extensions of the AP Stylebook, but exclusively covering local names, preferred terms and correct spelling of easily misspelled words relevant to the area.

I developed a local style sheet for a small newspaper a few years ago. Included were the correct name of a popular downtown restaurant that reporters constantly spelled several different ways; the full names and party affiliation of local politicians; acronyms for area organizations; and that the term "log truck," not "logging truck," was preferred.

A style sheet for your business or organization as an internal public relations writing reference should be developed and updated regularly. It should contain the proper names and titles of all employees, preferred spellings for industry jargon and anything else that might be easily confused or assumed to be correct when it's not.

Encourage others to review your style sheet and suggest corrections and additions.

ADD THE STYLE SHEET TO YOUR SPELL-CHECKING

When your own style sheet is completed, spend some time to add its entries to your word processor's spell-checker. This will greatly increase its functionality. A hard copy printout of the style sheet should be readily at hand and available to all members of your organization in both paper and computer file formats.

At a newspaper where I once worked, to my dismay I found whenever my last name would appear in a piece written by another reporter, it would invariably be misspelled. Unfortunately, that paper used old newswriting software that didn't include a spell-checking function.

NOTHING LASTS FOREVER

Hard-copy reference materials are prone to become outdated within a few years of publication and will need to be replaced with more current editions, but most of the resources listed in this chapter should enjoy a decent lifespan on your bookshelf.

It's also pretty handy to just pick up something like the AP Stylebook or a dictionary close at hand, without having to go to another program on your computer.

Reference software that is resident on your computer's hard drive and doesn't require a trip to the Internet also works well. The two Microsoft reference software programs – the *Encarta Reference Library* and *Streets and Trips* – have proven invaluable to me and are easy to use. While the Encarta encyclopedia's articles aren't particularly deep and there are many times when it simply won't have the entry you're looking for, it can't be beat for the price and ease of use.

LOVE THE INTERNET; HATE THE INTERNET

Information research has changed dramatically in the last 20 years, mostly for the better. The sole local telephone book and a massive city directory used to be must-haves for reporters. Now there are many competing local telephone books, and a name or business you need may not be in all of them.

The once-indispensable city directory has pretty much gone the way of the dinosaur, and no longer exists for most places.

But now we have the Internet, offering an unprecedented treasure trove of information via search engines like Google or Yahoo! The only problem is some of that information is incorrect – malicious gossip or opinion masquerading as fact.

You usually can trust Web sites run by Western governments and major news services, but everything else is suspect. Sad to say, even those government and news sites often contain politically influenced reports and biased news stories.

Like most things in life, you're pretty much on your own when it comes to quality control of information you use.

Internet blogs and bulletin boards are OK for entertainment or checking on a possible purchase, but are fairly useless for journalistic endeavors. Don't trust them at all.

I often use the Wikipedia free online encyclopedia, especially to guide me toward other reference sources. But Wikipedia has the same problems as the rest of the Internet, with tons of bad information finding its way onto your monitor.

A SAMPLE REFERENCE SHELF:

Here is a list of the reference works I keep next to my computer or on a nearby shelf in my home office. There are style guides, public relations manuals, journalism textbooks – even a World Almanac.

Most or all are in print at the time of this writing, but I'm always shocked to see how much textbooks cost. If you're on budget, stick to the general reference works.

PRINTED REFERENCE WORKS:

- **Local White and Yellow Pages** – obtain several competing directories
- **The Elements of Style** – Strunk and White, Macmillan
- **The World Almanac and Book of Facts (for current year)** – World Almanac Books
- **The Synonym Finder** – Rodale Press, Inc.
- **The Doubleday Roget's Thesaurus in Dictionary Form** – Doubleday & Company
- **Maps of your city, county, state, nation, the world**
- **Books and periodicals covering your own industry or profession**

MANUALS AND TEXTBOOKS:

- **News Writing** – George A. Hough, Houghton Mifflin Company

- **This is PR – The Realities of Public Relations** – Newsom, Scott and Turk, Wadsworth Publishing Company

- **Feature Writing for Newspapers & Magazines** – Friedlander and Lee, Harper Collins College Publishers

- **The Art and Craft of Feature Writing** – William E. Blundell, New American Library

- **Public Relations Writing, Form & Style** – Newsom and Carrell, Wadsworth, Inc.

- **Libel – Rights, Risks, Responsibilities** – Phelps and Hamilton, Dover Publications

- **Media Writing – Preparing Information for the Mass Media** – Newsom and Wollert, Wadsworth Publishing Company

- **Media/Impact – An Introduction to Mass Media** – Shirley Biagi, Wadsworth Publishing Company

- **Public Relations Handbook** – Dilenschneider and Forrestal, The Dartnell Corporation

- **The Art of Editing** – Baskette, Sissors and Brooks, Macmillan Publishing Company

- **The Complete Reporter -- Fundamentals of News Gathering, Writing and Editing** – Harriss, Leiter and Johnson, Macmillan Publishing Company

- **Inside Reporting – A Practical Guide to the Craft of Journalism** – Tim Harrower, McGraw-Hill

- **The Rights of Reporters** – Joel M. Gora, Discus Books

SOFTWARE

- **Street Atlas USA PLUS** – DeLorme (two DVDs) A mapping program that also contains searchable U.S. and Canadian business and white page telephone and address listings

CHAPTER 18
<u>STYLEBOOK QUIZZES</u>

By now, you've already learned that familiarity with "The Associated Press Stylebook" is necessary to produce professional new releases and other public relations.

But you shouldn't have to crack open the Associated Press Stylebook every time you write a few paragraphs. With regular use, the terms you commonly use will become second nature. Better yet, the reasoning behind many of the Stylebook's conventions will become part of your own intellectual map and you'll know how to follow AP style without picking up the book.

Learning by doing is definitely the way to hammer home the AP Stylebook. Reinforce its rules by using it for *all* your writing, not just public relations documents. E-mails, business and personal correspondence, school homework and even fiction writing will benefit by adhering to AP style.

Don't get too comfortable, though, because the AP Stylebook is updated regularly with new terms every few years and deletions of others. On rare occasions, an entry is changed to reflect common usage or new developments.

TRY THE QUIZZES

Following are a dozen quizzes on AP Stylebook entries. These are the same tests I used in teaching basic high school and college reporting classes, and are similar to the quizzes I faced as a journalism student.

Try reading the specific letter chapters of the AP Stylebook, then testing how well you've learned the information by taking a closed-book, multiple-choice quiz on those letters.

Most of the quizzes cover two letters – for example, A and B, C and D, etc. – with the exception of the quiz that spans six of the least-used letters, from U through Z, and the final quiz, which involves Internet and technology terms.

Note that the quizzes are in nonproportional `Courier` font – just like your news releases should be – in order to avoid any confusion regarding characters or spacing.

AN ANSWER KEY IS AT THE END OF THIS CHAPTER

As mentioned, the AP Stylebook changes over time – Don't be surprised if the entries for a few quiz questions have dropped out of the latest edition.

CIRCLE THE LETTER OF THE CORRECT ANSWER (only one answer is correct)

1. a. The Roman general died in A.D. 96.
    b. The Roman general died in 96 A.D.

2. a. They met at 1313 E. Fifth Street.
    b. They met at 1313 E. 5th St.
    c. They met at 1313 East Fifth Street.
    d. They met at 1313 East 5th St.
    e. They met at 1313 E. 5th Street.
    f. They met at 1313 E. Fifth St.

3. a. He was a special adviser: his role was strictly advisory.
    b. He was a special adviser: his role was strictly advisery.
    c. He was a special advisor: his role was strictly advisory.
    d. He was a special advisor: his role was strictly advisery.

4. a. The plane belonged to Air India.
    b. The plane belonged to AirIndia.
    c. The plane belonged to Air-India.
    d. The plane belonged to Air India Airlines.

5. a. He alluded to the criminal by first name only.
    b. He referred to the criminal by first name only.

6. a. The three men divided the loot between them.
    b. The three men divided the loot among them.

7. a. She said she was from Tucson, Arizona, en route to Austin, Texas.
    b. She said she was from Tucson, Ariz., en route to Austin, Texas.
    c. She said she was from Tucson, AZ, en route to Austin, TX.

8. a. The news was delivered by U.S. Embassy attache Robert P. Smith.
    b. The news was delivered by U.S. Embassy Attache Robert P. Smith.

9. a. The president gave out special ball point pens.
    b. The president gave out special ballpoint pens.

10. a. He is a blonde; she is a blonde.
    b. He is blond; she is blonde.
    c. He is blond; she is a blonde.
    d. He is blonde; she is blond.

11. a. They did not know the phone was tapped.
    b. They did not know the room was tapped.

12 a. Incredibly, his shot hit the bull's-eye of the target.
    b. Incredibly, his shot hit the bullseye of the target.
    c. Incredibly, his shot hit the bulls-eye of the target.
    d. Incredibly, his shot hit the bull's eye of the target.

13 a. A biennial festival, it was held every two years.
    b. A biannual festival, it was held every two years.

###

CIRCLE THE LETTER OF THE CORRECT ANSWER (only one answer is correct)

1. a. He is a native of The Camerouns.
    b. He is a native of Cameroon.
    c. He is a native of Cameroun.
    d. He is a native of Cameroons.

2. a. The food was covered with Cellophane.
    b. The food was covered with cellophane.

3. a. The car collided with a utility pole.
    b. The car collided with an oncoming truck.
    c. The car collided with a parked truck.

4. a. Nancy Jones, the feminist comedienne, was featured.
    b. Nancy Jones, the feminist comedian, was featured.

5. a. The house was totally destroyed by the fire.
    b. The house was destroyed by the fire.
    c. The house was completely destroyed by the fire.
    d. The house was partially destroyed by the fire.

6. a. They tried to coverup the scandal.
    b. They tried to cover-up the scandal.
    c. They tried to cover up the scandal.

7. a. She claimed it was the work of the Devil.
    b. She claimed it was the work of satan.
    c. She claimed it was the work of the devil.

8. a. Alone on the lake, the boy fell through the ice and drowned.
    b. Alone on the lake, the boy fell through the ice and was drowned.

9. a. The hat compliments her dress.
    b. The hat complements her dress.

10. a. Yesterday's invasion began in the Canal Zone.
    b. Yesterday's invasion began in the Panama Canal Zone.
    c. Yesterday's invasion began in the Panama canal zone.
    d. Yesterday's invasion began in the U.S. Canal zone.

11. a. They loved their citizen's band radio.
    b. They loved their Citizens Band radio.
    c. They loved their citizens band radio.
    d. They loved their Citizens' band radio.

12. a. She was diagnosed using a CAT scan.
    b. She was diagnosed using a CAT-scan.
    c. She was diagnosed using a C-T scan.
    d. She was diagnosed using a CT scan.
    e. She was diagnosed using a C.A.T. scan.
    f. She was diagnosed using a C.T. scan.

###

CIRCLE THE LETTER OF THE CORRECT ANSWER (only one answer is correct)

1.   a.   The tremblor measured 7.1 on the Richter scale.
       b.   The temblor measured 7.1 on the Richter scale.

2.   a.   She interviewed Editor-in-Chief Horace Greeley.
       b.   She interviewed Editor in Chief Horace Greeley.
       c.   She interviewed editor in chief Horace Greeley.
       d.   She interviewed editor-in-chief Horace Greeley.

3.   a.   Steps were taken to insure accuracy.
       b.   Steps were taken to ensure accuracy.

4.   a.   They lived with Eskimoes for several years.
       b.   They lived with Eskimos for several years.

5.   a.   The group depended on Federal assistance.
       b.   The group depended on federal assistance.

6.   a.   The first family of the United States lives in the White House.
       b.   The First Family of the United States lives in the White House.

7.   a.   The editor claimed to be French-Canadian.
       b.   The editor claimed to be French Canadian.
       c.   The editor claimed to be French-Canadien.

8.   a.   He forsook his desire to visit a fortune-teller.
       b.   He forsaked his desire to visit a fortune teller.
       c.   He forsook his desire to visit a fortuneteller.
       d.   He forsaked his desire to visit a fortune-teller.

9.   a.   The victim died enroute to the hospital.
       b.   The victim died en route to the hospital.

10.   a.   Julie and her only husband David went shopping.
       b.   Julie and her only husband, David, went shopping.

11.   a.   Neither they nor he is going.
       b.   Neither he nor they is going.
       c.   Neither they nor he are going.

12.   a.   The filibuster, Sen. Adams, started the filibuster.
       b.   The filibusterer, Sen. Adams, started the filibuster.
       c.   The filibustor, Sen. Adams, started the filibuster.

13.   a.   Her dream was to be a freelance writer.
       b.   Her dream was to be a free-lance writer.

14.   a.   The two intruders looked at one another.
       b.   The two intruders looked at each other.

###

CIRCLE THE LETTER OF THE CORRECT ANSWER (only one answer is correct)

1. a. He was forced to run a gantlet of criticism.
    b. He was forced to run a gauntlet of criticism.
    c. He was forced to run a gauntelet of criticism.

2. a. The gourmand always ate very small meals.
    b. The gourmet always ate very small meals.

3. a. "Don't give me that gobbledygook," he said.
    b. "Don't give me that Gobbledygook," he said.
    c. "Don't give me that gobbledegook," he said.
    d. "Don't give me that Gobbledegook," he said.

4. a. It was the first visit by Governor Rose Mofford.
    b. It was the first visit by governor Rose Mofford.
    c. It was the first visit by Gov. Rose Mofford.

5. a. The Northern Plains are part of the Great Plains.
    b. The northern plains are part of the Great Plains.
    c. The northern Plains are part of the Great Plains.

6. a. He is considered very-well-educated and widely-read.
    b. He is considered very well-educated and widely read.
    c. He is considered very well educated and widely read.

7. a. She halfheartedly told her half brother a half-truth.
    b. She half-heartedly told her half-brother a half-truth.
    c. She halfheartedly told her half-brother a half truth.
    d. She half-heartedly told her half brother a half-truth.

8. a. After his wife died, the widower lacked motivation to live.
    b. After his wife died, the husband lacked motivation to live.

9. a. He received a 10- to 20-year sentence in prison.
    b. He received a 10-to-20-year sentence in prison.
    c. He received a 10-to 20-year sentence in prison.

10. a. The man believed in one god, and said he was obedient to him.
    b. The man believed in one God, and said he was obedient to him.
    c. The man believed in one God, and said he was obedient to Him.

11. a. The protest blocked Interstate highway 19.
    b. The protest blocked Interstate Highway I-19.
    c. The protest blocked Interstate Highway 19.

12. a. A hydrogen bomb is probably too complex for terrorists to produce.
    b. An H-bomb is probably too complex for terrorists to produce.
    c. An h-bomb is probably too complex for terrorists to produce.

###

CIRCLE THE LETTER OF THE CORRECT ANSWER (only one answer is correct)

1.   a.   Raccoon coats are "in" again.
     b.   Raccoon coats are in again.
     c.   Raccoon coats are In again.
     d.   Raccoon coats are "In" again.

2.   a.   The researcher feared the planet was entering another Ice Age.
     b.   The researcher feared the planet was entering another ice age.

3.   a.   The IndoGerman was from IndoChina.
     b.   The Indo-German was from Indo-China.
     c.   The Indo German was from Indochina.
     d.   The Indo-German was from Indochina.
     e.   The Indogerman was from Indo-china.
     f.   The IndoGerman was from Indo-China.

4.   a.   The ground shook like jello.
     b.   The ground shook like Jello.
     c.   The ground shook like Jell-O.
     d.   The ground shook like jell-o.

5.   The photograph was clearly J.P. Kennedy, Jr.
     a.   He played around on his Jet Ski all summer.
     b.   He played around on his Jetski all summer.
     c.   He played around on his Jet-Ski all summer.
     d.   He played around on his JetSki all summer.

6.   a.   The author was U.S. District Judge John J. Sirica.
     b.   The author was U.S. District Court Judge John J. Sirica.

7.   a.   He worked part time as a Jehovah's Witnesses pioneer.
     b.   He worked part time as a Jehovah's Witness regular pioneer.
     c.   He worked part time as a Jehovah's Witnesses regular pioneer.
     d.   He worked part time as a Jehovah's Witness pioneer.

8.   a.   I once knew a man from the Island of Nantucket.
     b.   I once knew a man from the island of Nantucket.

9.   a.   The Iranian student spoke only Farsi.
     b.   The Iranian student spoke only Iranian.

10. a.   The ship crossed the international date line.
     b.   The ship crossed the International Date Line.

11. a.   She said all children in public schools should be innoculated.
     b.   She said all children in public schools should be inoculated.
     c.   She said all children in public schools should be innocullated.
     d.   She said all children in public schools should be inocullated.

###

Circle the letter of the correct answer (only one answer is correct)

1. a.   "It's a Kris Kringle suit," he said.
    b.   "It's a Chris Kringle suit," he said.
    c.   "It's a Kriss Kringle suit," he said.

2. a.   The whole family belonged to the Ku Kux Klan.
    b.   The whole family belonged to the Klu Kux Klan.
    c.   The whole family belonged to the Klu Klux Klan.
    d.   The whole family belonged to the Ku Klux Klan.

3. a.   The horse trader was from Lexington, Ken.
    b.   The horse trader was from Lexington, Kty.
    c.   The horse trader was from Lexington, Ky.
    d.   The horse trader was from Lexington, Kentucky.
    e.   The horse trader was from Lexington, KY.

4. a.   The Kansas City, Kansas, store sold lanolin soap.
    b.   The Kansas City, Ka., sold Lanolin soap.
    c.   The Kansas City, KS, store sold Lanolin soap.
    d.   The Kansas City, Kan., store sold lanolin soap.

5. a.   K-Mart had the best price.
    b.   Kmart had the best price.
    c.   K-mart had the best price.

6. a.   The speaker stood behind the podium.
    b.   The speaker stood on the podium.
    c.   The speaker stood in the podium.

7. a.   I could see by her bright red face that she was livid with rage.
    b.   I could see by her dull purple face that she was livid with rage.
    c.   I could see by her dilated pupils that she was livid with rage.

8. a.   "You can read it in the Quran," Lt. Gov. Smith said.
    b.   "You can read it in the Koran." Lieutenant Governor Smith said.

9. a.   She would not let up in her criticism of the letup in funding.
    b.   She would not let-up in her criticism of the let up in funding.
    c.   She would not letup in her criticism of the let-up in funding.
    d.   She would not let up in her criticism of the let-up in funding.

10. a.   They created a likable life style.
    b.   They created a likeable life style.
    c.   They created a likable life-style.
    d.   They created a likable lifestyle.
    e.   They created a likeable life-style.
    f.   They created a likeable lifestyle.

11. a.   The mobster was addicted to candy, especially LifeSavers.
    b.   The mobster was addicted to candy, especially Life Savers.
    c.   The mobster was addicted to candy, especially Lifesavers.
    d.   The mobster was addicted to candy, especially Life-Savers.

###

CIRCLE THE LETTER OF THE CORRECT ANSWER (only one answer is correct)

1.   a.   He was awarded the Congressional Medal of Honor.
      b.   He was awarded the Medal of Honor.

2.   a.   The store specializes in mens wear.
      b.   The store specializes in mens' wear.
      c.   The store specializes in men's wear.
      d.   The store specializes in menswear.

3.   a.   She smuggled 12 centimeters of 35-millimeter film.
      b.   She smuggled 12 centimeters of 35mm film.
      c.   She smuggled 12cm of 35mm film.
      d.   She smuggled 12 centimeters of 35 mm film.
      e.   She smuggled 12 centimeters of 35-mm film.

4.   a.   At midsemester, they found themselves in the midAtlantic.
      b.   At midsemester, they found themselves in the mid-Atlantic.
      c.   At mid-semester, they found themselves in the mid-Atlantic.

5.   a.   The speaker was First Sergeant Alvin C. York from Fort Huachuca.
      b.   The speaker was 1st. Sgt. Alvin C. York from Fort Huachuca.
      c.   The speaker was First Sgt. Alvin C. York from Fort Huachuca.
      d.   The speaker was 1st Sgt. Alvin C. York from Fort Huachuca.
      e.   The speaker was First Sargent Alvin C. York from Fort Huachuca.
      f.   The speaker was 1st Sargent Alvin C. York from Fort Huachuca.

6.   a.   The invention turned out to be a real moneymaker.
      b.   The invention turned out to be a real money maker.
      c.   The invention turned out to be a real money-maker.

7.   a.   January 1972 was a cold month.
      b.   January, 1972, was a cold month.

8.   a.   The mosquitoes droned on all night.
      b.   The mosquitos droned on all night.

9.   a.   "It's a case of Murphy's Law," he said.
      b.   "It's a case of Murphy's law," he said.

10.   a.   Her multicolored dress stood out in a crowd.
      b.   Her multi-colored dress stood out in a crowd.

11.   a.   "Let's mop-up," was the slogan of the mopup operation.
      b.   "Let's mop up," was the slogan of the mop-up operation.
      c.   "Let's mop-up," was the slogan of the mop up operation.
      d.   "Let's mopup," was the slogan of the mop-up operation.

12.   a.   She is the president of the National Governors' Association.
      b.   She is the president of the National Governors Association.
      c.   She is the president of the National Governor's Association.

(more M and N quiz on following page)

13. a. The couch was redone in naugahyde.
     b. The couch was redone in naugahide.
     c. The couch was redone in Naugahyde.
     d. The couch was redone in Naugahide.

14. a. He was Coach Frankie's number one player.
     b. He was Coach Frankie's number 1 player.
     c. He was Coach Frankie's Number One player.
     d. He was Coach Frankie's Number 1 player.
     e. He was Coach Frankie's No. One player.
     f. He was Coach Frankie's No. 1 player.

15. a. The cafeteria became a sort of no-man's land.
     b. The cafeteria became a sort of no-man's-land.
     c. The cafeteria became a sort of no man's land.
     d. The cafeteria became a sort of no man's-land.

16. a. He was so nondescript, he became a nonperson.
     b. He was so non-descript, he became a non-person.
     c. He was so nondescript, he became a non-person.
     d. He was so non-descript, he became a nonperson.

17. a. None of the seats were correctly placed.
     b. None of the seats was correctly placed.

18. a. It became a nationwide epidemic.
     b. It became a nation-wide epidemic.

19. a. The priest celebrated High Mass.
     b. The priest celebrated high Mass.
     c. The priest celebrated high mass.

20. a. Pima College uses the very cheapest mimeograph machines.
     b. Pima College uses the very cheapest Mimeograph machines.

21. a. The corner news stand had shut down.
     b. The corner newstand had shut down.
     c. The corner newsstand had shut down.

22. a. The Methodist bishop presided over a large bishopric.
     b. The Methodist bishop presided over a large diocese.
     c. The Methodist bishop presided over a large church area.
     d. The Methodist bishop presided over a large denominationality.
     e. The Methodist bishop presided over a large catechumen.

###

CIRCLE THE LETTER OF THE CORRECT ANSWER (only one answer is correct)

1.　a.　He said the proposal was O.K.
　　b.　He said the proposal was okay.
　　c.　He said the proposal was OK.

2.　a.　She referred to the photo on page nine.
　　b.　She referred to the photo on Page nine.
　　c.　She referred to the photo on p. 9.
　　d.　She referred to the photo on Page 9.
　　e.　She referred to the photo on page 9.

3.　a.　She works part-time. She has a part-time job.
　　b.　She works parttime. She has a part-time job.
　　c.　She works part time. She has a parttime job.
　　d.　She works part time. She has a part-time job.
　　e.　She works part-time. She has a part time job.

4.　a.　The milk apparently had not been Pasteurized.
　　b.　The milk apparently had not been pasteurized.

5.　a.　The raise amounted to one percent.
　　b.　The raise amounted to 1 percent.
　　c.　The raise amounted to 1%.
　　d.　The raise amounted to 1-percent.
　　e.　The raise amounted to one-percent.

6.　a.　The sign read: "John Smith, Ph.d."
　　b.　The sign read: "John Smith, Ph.D."
　　c.　The sign read: "John Smith, ph.d."
　　d.　The sign read: "John Smith, PH.D."

7.　a.　The ball went out-of-bounds.
　　b.　The ball went out of bounds.

8.　a.　He pled guilty to the charge.
　　b.　He pleaded guilty to the charge.

9.　a.　They settled their argument with a game of ping pong.
　　b.　They settled their argument with a game of ping-pong.
　　c.　They settled their argument with a game of pingpong.

10.　a.　The budget cuts eliminated the team's pom-pom girls.
　　b.　The budget cuts eliminated the team's pompon girls.
　　c.　The budget cuts eliminated the team's pom pom girls.

11.　a.　They ignored the hostess's invitation.
　　b.　They ignored the hostess' invitation.

12.　a.　They stole the hostess's seat.
　　b.　They stole the hostess' seat.

(more O and P quiz on following page)

13.   a.   On Tuesdays, the guru would prophesy prophecies.
        b.   On Tuesdays, the guru would prophesy prophesies.
        c.   On Tuesdays, the guru would prophecy prophesies.
        d.   On Tuesdays, the guru would prophecy prophecies.

14.   a.   The odds-maker was odd-looking.
        b.   The odds-maker was odd looking.
        c.   The oddsmaker was odd-looking.
        d.   The odds maker was odd-looking.
        e.   The odds maker was oddlooking.
        f.   The oddsmaker was odd looking.

15.   a.   The oldtimer's stories were all lies.
        b.   The old-timer's stories were all lies.

16.   a.   She called the plea bargain a cop-out.
        b.   She called the plea bargain a copout.
        c.   She called the plea bargain a cop out.

17.   a.   It was an expensive oriental rug.
        b.   It was an expensive Oriental rug.

18.   a.   Doctors installed a Pacemaker in his chest.
        b.   Doctors installed a pacemaker in his chest.

19.   a.   He was a victim of Parkinson's Disease.
        b.   He was a victim of Parkinson's disease.

20.   a.   Man could not survive in the Martian atmosphere.
        b.   Man could not survive in the martian atmosphere.

21.   a.   Thousands watched the Pontiff arrive.
        b.   Thousands watched the pontiff arrive.

22.   a.   It was a violent post-election period.
        b.   It was a violent postelection period.

23.   a.   The accident happened in the pre-dawn darkness.
        b.   The accident happened in the predawn darkness.

24.   a.   "Express that in pre-tax income," he said.
        b.   "Express that in pretax income," he said.

25.   a.   The formula is: Two parts powder to eleven parts water.
        b.   The formula is: Two parts powder to 11 parts water.
        c.   The formula is: 2 parts powder to 11 parts water.

###

CIRCLE THE LETTER OF THE CORRECT ANSWER (only one answer is correct)

1. a.   Q: "Where did you keep it?"
         A: "In a little tin box."
    b.   Q: Where did you keep it?
         A: In a little tin box.

2. a.   He flew to Sydney on Qantas.
    b.   He flew to Sydney on Qantas Airlines.
    c.   He flew to Sydney on Quantas.
    d.   He flew to Sydney on Quantas Airlines.
    e.   He flew to Sydney on Qantas Airways.
    f.   He flew to Sydney on Quantas Airways.
    g.   He flew to Sydney on Qantas Air Lines.
    h.   He flew to Sydney on Quantas Air Lines.

3. a.   The murder weapon was a tennis racquet.
    b.   The murder weapon was a tennis racket.

4. a.   The ratio was 2-to-1.
    b.   It was a 2-to-1 ratio.

5. a.   She found his charms supremely resistable.
    b.   She found his charms supremely resistible.

6. a.   The rescission of the treaty generated much dismay.
    b.   The recision of the treaty generated much dismay.
    c.   The recission of the treaty generated much dismay.

7. a.   She works for Reuters; she is a Reuters correspondent.
    b.   She works for Reuters; she is a Reuter correspondent.
    c.   She works for Reuter; she is a Reuter's correspondent.
    d.   She works for Reuter; she is a Reuter correspondent.

8. a.   Give me that good old rock-n-roll.
    b.   Give me that good old rock 'n roll.
    c.   Give me that good old rock and roll.
    d.   Give me that good old rock 'n' roll.
    e.   Give me that good old rock-and-roll.

9. a.   Let's round-up the cows for the roundup.
    b.   Let's round up the cows for the roundup.
    c.   Let's roundup the cows for the round-up.
    d.   Let's round up the cows for the round-up.

10. a.   "The rules were designed to keep out the riff-raff," he said.
    b.   "The rules were designed to keep out the riff raff," he said.
    c.   "The rules were designed to keep out the riffraff," he said.

11. a.   He rifled through the pages of the book, looking for the photo.
    b.   He riffled through the pages of the book, looking for the photo.

###

(CIRCLE THE LETTER OF THE CORRECT ANSWER (only one answer is correct)

1. a. It was the second time the city's sewerage system had failed.
   b. It was the second time the city's sewage system had failed.
   c. It was the second time the city's sewer system had failed.

2. a. The storm had torn away most of the sheetrock.
   b. The storm had torn away most of the Sheetrock.

3. a. The Space age began Oct. 4, 1957.
   b. The space Age began Oct. 4, 1957.
   c. The Space Age began Oct. 4, 1957.

4. a. The remote control had a touchscreen display.
   b. The remote control had a touch-screen display.

5. a. They gave away anything that was not saleable.
   b. They gave away anything that was not salable.

6. a. She was a well-known sculptress.
   b. She was a well-known sculptor.

7. a. The president met Abul Nari, secretary of state of Burundi.
   b. The president met Abul Nari, Secretary of State of Burundi.

8. a. He viewed the agreement as a sell out.
   b. He viewed the agreement as a sell-out.
   c. He viewed the agreement as a sellout.

9. a. They gave away anything that was not serviceable.
   b. They gave away anything that was not servicable.

10. a. The sesquicentennial was celebrated every 75 years.
    b. The sesquicentennial was celebrated every 50 years.
    c. The sesquicentennial was celebrated every 150 years.

11. a. It was a sizeable increase.
    b. It was a sizable increase.

12. a. Her boyfriend looked a lot like Smoky the Bear.
    b. Her boyfriend looked a lot like Smoky Bear.
    c. Her boyfriend looked a lot like Smokey the Bear.
    d. Her boyfriend looked a lot like Smokey Bear.

13. a. "The Star-Spangled Banner" is the National Anthem.
    b. "The Star-Spangled Banner" is the national anthem.

14. a. He staunched the flow of blood.
    b. He stanched the flow of blood.
    c. He stinched the flow of blood.

(more S and T quiz on following page)

15.   a.   "I'm looking for a size 44-long straitjacket," he said.
         b.   "I'm looking for a size 44-long straightjacket," he said.
         c.   "I'm looking for a size 44-long strait jacket," he said.
         d.   "I'm looking for a size 44-long straight jacket," he said.
         e.   "I'm looking for a size 44-long straight-jacket," he said.
         f.   "I'm looking for a size 44-long strait-jacket," he said.

16.   a.   The overworked and underpaid instructor prepared 30 syllabuses.
         b.   The overworked and underpaid instructor prepared 30 syllabi.

17.   a.   She worked for a supra-governmental agency.
         b.   She worked for a supragovernmental agency.

18.   a.   Luckily, we caught a tail wind.
         b.   Luckily, we caught a tailwind.

19.   a.   The weatherman could perform only with the aid of a teleprompter.
         b.   The weatherman could perform only with the aid of a Teleprompter.
         c.   The weatherman could perform only with the aid of a TelePrompTer.
         d.   The weatherman could perform only with the aid of a Tele-Prompter.

20.   a.   The company reported a ten-fold increase in profits.
         b.   The company reported a tenfold increase in profits.
         c.   The company reported a 10-fold increase in profits.

21.   a.   The day's low was minus 10.
         b.   The day's low was -10.

22.   a.   "I feel in tip-top shape," were the general's last words.
         b.   "I feel in tip top shape," were the general's last words.
         c.   "I feel in tiptop shape," were the general's last words.

23.   a.   The killer moved toward the gas chamber.
         b.   The killer moved towards the gas chamber.

24.   a.   Aunt Mamie presented a boring travelog of her trip to Iowa.
         b.   Aunt Mamie presented a boring travelogue of her trip to Iowa.

25.   a.   The statuary depicted Jesus and the 12 Apostles.
         b.   The statuary depicted Jesus and the Twelve Apostles.
         c.   The statuary depicted Jesus and the 12 apostles.

26.   a.   The senator called the bill a trojan horse.
         b.   The senator called the bill a Trojan Horse.
         c.   The senator called the bill a Trojan horse.

27.   a.   The bottle contained 40 teaspoonsful.
         b.   The bottle contained 40 teaspoonfuls.

###

(Circle the letter of the correct answer. Only one answer is correct)

1. a.   He charmed all the girls with his virtuoso ukelele playing.
   b.   He charmed all the girls with his virtuoso ukulele playing.

2. a.   The naval maneuvers are underway.
   b.   The naval maneuvers are under way.

3. a.   She looked upwards into the elevator shaft.
   b.   She looked upward into the elevator shaft.

4. a.   It was the blue team versus the reds.
   b.   It was the blue team vs. the reds.
   c.   It was the blue team verses the reds.

5. a.   The governor handed down few vetos.
   b.   The governor handed down few vetoes.

6. a.   The vice-principal became annoyed.
   b.   The vice principal became annoyed.

7. a.   They breakfasted on vienna sausages.
   b.   They breakfasted on Vienna sausages.

8. a.   He preferred v-neck sweaters.
   b.   He preferred vee-neck sweaters.
   c.   He preferred V-neck sweaters.

9. a.   Her looks were considered a real votegetter.
   b.   Her looks were considered a real vote-getter.
   c.   Her looks were considered a real vote getter.

10. a.   "I'll never understand this voicemail system," she said.
    b.   "I'll never understand this voice mail system," she said.
    c.   "I'll never understand this voice-mail system," she said.

11. a.   It was a .50-caliber Browning machine gun.
    b.   It was a 50-caliber Browning machine gun.
    c.   It was a 50-cal. Browning machine gun.
    d.   It was a .50-cal. Browning machine gun.
    e.   It was a 0.50-caliber Browning machine gun.

12. a.   They slept in the weatherbeaten old barn.
    b.   They slept in the weather-beaten old barn.

13. a.   Nearshore waters extend to one mile from shore.
    b.   Nearshore waters extend to three miles from shore.
    c.   Nearshore waters extend to five miles from shore.
    d.   Nearshore waters extend to 10 miles from shore.

14. a.   His whereabouts are a mystery.
    b.   His whereabouts is a mystery.

(more U to Z quiz on following page)

15. a.   He practically lived on Scotch whisky.
      b.   He practically lived on Scotch whiskey.

16. a.   She wore a maroon windbreaker.
      b.   She wore a maroon Windbreaker.
      c.   She wore a maroon Wind-Breaker.
      d.   She wore a maroon Wind breaker.

17. a.   The scene was a windswept plateau.
      b.   The scene was a wind-swept plateau.

18. a.   She was somewhat unique in her skills at video games.
      b.   She was very unique in her skills at videogames.
      c.   She was unique in her skills at video-games.
      d.   She was unique in her skills at videogames.
      e.   She was unique in her skills at video games.
      f.   She was somewhat unique in her skills at videogames.
      g.   She was very unique in her skills at video games.
      h.   She was somewhat unique in her skills at video-games.

19. a.   He was a worshiper of the rat god, Utalek.
      b.   He was a worshipper of the rat god, Utalek.

20. a.   He had one passion in life: the Yo-Yo.
      b.   He had one passion in life: the yo-yo.
      c.   He had one passion in life: the yoyo.

21. a.   I wish you loads of Yuletide cheer.
      b.   I wish you loads of yuletide cheer.

22. a.   The vessel followed a zig-zag pattern.
      b.   The vessel followed a zigzag pattern.

23. a.   She could not remember her ZIP Code.
      b.   She could not remember her Zipcode.
      c.   She could not remember her Zip code.
      d.   She could not remember her ZIP CODE.
      e.   She could not remember her ZIP code.
      f.   She could not remember her zipcode.
      g.   She could not remember her ZIPCODE.

24. a.   He still has nightmares of Vietnam.
      b.   He still has nightmares of Viet Nam.
      c.   He still has nightmares of Viet-Nam.

25. a.   He practically lived on Bourbon whiskey.
      b.   He practically lived on Bourbon whisky.

26. a.   George H.W. Bush often was called the "Velcro president."
      b.   George H.W. Bush often was called the "velcro president."

###

CIRCLE THE LETTER OF THE CORRECT ANSWER (only one answer is correct)

1.   a.   She invested in a dot.com company that failed.
       b.   She invested in a dot-com company that failed.
       c.   She invested in a dotcom company that failed.
       d.   She invested in a dot com company that failed.

2.   a.   The news release was sent via E-mail.
       b.   The news release was sent via email.
       c.   The news release was sent via e-mail.

3.   a.   "This computer is a data processing miracle," he said.
       b.   "This computer is a data-processing miracle," he said.

4.   a.   He could access his Intranet from the internet.
       b.   He could access his intranet from the internet.
       c.   He could access his intranet from the Internet.
       d.   He could access his Intranet from the Internet.

5.   a.   "I wish I had a website," she said.
       b.   "I wish I had a web site," she said.
       c.   "I wish I had a Website," she said.
       d.   "I wish I had a Web site," she said.

6.   a.   Online shopping was easy for them.
       b.   On-line shopping was easy for them.

7.   a.   It was hard to log-in, log-on and log-off on that computer.
       b.   It was hard to log in, log on and log off on that computer.
       c.   It was hard to login, logon and logoff on that computer.

8.   a.   He had the world's most boring screensaver.
       b.   He had the world's most boring screen saver.

9.   a.   The webcast mentioned our Web page.
       b.   The Webcast mentioned our Webpage.
       c.   The web cast mentioned our web page.
       d.   The Web cast mentioned our Web page.

10.   a.   They could not think of a good Domain name.
       b.   They could not think of a good Domain.name.
       c.   They could not think of a good domain name.
       d.   They could not think of a good domainname.

11.   a.   Their romance began in Cyberspace.
       b.   Their romance began in cyberspace.
       c.   Their romance began in cyber-space.
       d.   Their romance began in Cyber-space.
       b.   Their romance began in CyberSpace.
       c.   Their romance began in Cyber-Space.

###

AP Stylebook quizzes answer key:

A and B: 1-a, 2-f, 3-a, 4-c, 5-b, 6-b, 7-b, 8-a, 9-a, 10-c, 11-a, 12-a, 13-a

C & D: 1-b, 2-b, 3-b, 4-b, 5-b, 6-c, 7-c, 8-a, 9-b, 10-c, 11-d, 12-d

E & F: 1-b, 2-a, 3-b, 4-b, 5-b, 6-a, 7-b, 8-c, 9-b, 10-b, 11-a, 12-a, 13-a, 14-b

G & H: 1-a, 2-b, 3-a, 4-c, 5-c, 6-b, 7-a, 8-b, 9-a, 10-b, 11-c, 12-a

I & J: 1-b, 2-b, 3-d, 4-c, 5-b, 6-b, 7-a, 8-c, 9-b, 10-a, 11-a, 12-b

K & L: 1-c, 2-d, 3-c, 4-d, 5-b, 6-b, 7-b, 8-a, 9-a, 10-d, 11-b

M & N: 1-b, 2-d, 3-d, 4-b, 5-d, 6-a, 7-a, 8-a, 9-b, 10-a, 11-b, 12-b, 13-c, 14-f, 15-c, 16-b, 17-b, 18-a, 19-b, 20-a, 21-c, 22-c

O & P: 1-c, 2-d, 3-d, 4-b, 5-b, 6-b, 7-b, 8-b, 9-c, 10-b, 11-a, 12-b, 13-a, 14-c, 15-b, 16-a, 17-b, 18-b, 19-b, 20-a, 21-b, 22-b, 23-a, 24-b, 25-c

Q & R: 1-b, 2-e, 3-b, 4-a, 5-b, 6-a, 7-a, 8-d, 9-b, 10-c, 11-b

S & T: 1-b, 2-b, 3-c, 4-b, 5-b, 6-b, 7-a, 8-c, 9-a, 10-c, 11-b, 12-d, 13-b, 14-b, 15-a, 16-a, 17-b, 18-a, 19-a, 20-b, 21-a, 22-c, 23-a, 24-b, 25-b, 26-c, 27-b

U - Z: 1-b, 2-b, 3-b, 4-a, 5-b, 6-b, 7-a, 8-c, 9-b, 10-b, 11-a, 12-b, 13-c, 14-b, 15-a, 16-b, 17-b, 18-e, 19-b, 20-b, 21-b, 22-b, 23-e, 24-a, 25-a, 26-a

**INTERNET AND
TECHNOLOGY TERMS:**   1-b, 2-c, 3-a, 4-c, 5-d, 6-a, 7-b, 8-b, 9-a, 10-c, 11-b

YOU DID IT!

The preceding 18 chapters of this book could be considered a crash course in journalism – a field of study that usually entails at least four years of full-time college coursework and a lot of hands-on experience.

Even though the information was condensed down to the essentials, there still was a lot to digest and remember. Here are the important points from each chapter:

CHAPTER 1 – INTRODUCTION

- Chapters 4, 5 and 6 on writing, formatting and sending news releases form the practical core of this book.
- Public relations is gaining and maintaining positive public awareness, understanding and support by arranging favorable publicity.
- PR material must be newsworthy to be considered for submittal and publication.
- Successful PR placements in the media are virtually indistinguishable from news.
- Most stories in the media have PR origins.
- Public relations is cost-effective, particularly when compared to paid advertising.
- PR methods often are misused, resulting in a negative image for public relations practitioners.
- A public relations campaign usually involves much more than news releases.
- Honesty, brevity and newsworthiness pay off in the long run for PR efforts.

CHAPTER 2 – IN-HOUSE PUBLIC RELATIONS

- Most individuals and small offices have the talent and equipment to do most public relations services.
- Bosses and technical types probably are poor choices to write or edit material.
- A basic reporting class would be very beneficial.
- A basic computer and Internet setup is all that's needed for PR work.
- Use popular, widely adopted software for writing and digital image editing.
- Keep a dictionary and the *Associated Press Stylebook* close at hand.
- Be wary of Internet-origin information.
- Check your facts from many sources.

CHAPTER 3 – WHEN DO YOU NEED A NEWS RELEASE?

- News releases are news stories, in both form and purpose.
- Most of the material seen in print and broadcast news has its origins in public relations.
- The "newsworthiness" of your material – its importance to the audience, timeliness, accuracy and interest – will determine its chances in the media.
- Carefully consider if your information deserves a news release.
- Supplying information well in advance of an event helps the media.
- Don't use news releases for purposes better suited for paid advertising.

CHAPTER 4 – WRITING A NEWS RELEASE

- Learn to write in journalism style – short, simple and accurate.
- Follow the "inverted pyramid" construction.
- Summarize all important information in the first few paragraphs – the "lead."
- Learn the Associated Press Stylebook and use it as your primary reference.
- Keep it short: one page is best.
- Avoid suspense, sarcasm and other creative writing techniques.
- Always identify people completely. Don't use first names on second reference.
- Spelling and grammar errors leave a very bad impression.
- Proofreading by others is critical. Writers should not try to proofread their own work.
- Stick to simple punctuation, and learn how to punctuate correctly.
- Photo captions have their own set of rules and functions.

CHAPTER 5 – FORMATTING A NEWS RELEASE

- News release formatting follows traditional journalistic practice.
- E-mailed releases are formatted differently than hard copy versions.
- Composing with a word processor is easier and more flexible than trying to do everything within an e-mail program.
- Keep things simple and uncluttered.
- Always put release header, contacts, release date and editor's notes above the news release text.
- Hard copy formatting is more complicated than e-mails, with wide margins, monospaced fonts, double-spaced text and page continuations.

CHAPTER 6 – SENDING A NEWS RELEASE

- E-mail is by far the best way to submit PR materials. It's faster, cheaper and less hassle on the receiving end.
- Faxes and personal delivery work in certain circumstances.
- Photographs and graphics should be attachments. Inserting them into the body of the e-mail takes up too much space.
- Create media lists for your PR recipients by reading publication staff boxes and contacting media operations to find the best persons to contact.
- Constantly maintain your media list by checking and updating the contacts.
- Timing is important. Know the lead times for advance notice.
- Know the deadlines for various publications and broadcasts.

CHAPTER 7 – STAFF ANNOUNCEMENTS

- Present news about people in your organization.
- Are a staple of business sections and industry publications.
- Provide recognition and a morale boost to employees.
- Before interviewing, research the person featured.
- Attach a photograph of the people in the announcement whenever possible.

CHAPTER 8 – FACT SHEETS

- Can be included with news releases or in media kits.
- Keep to a single page.
- Review and update regularly. Keep current version handy.
- Can be produced for the business or organization, events and people.

CHAPTER 9 – FEATURES

- Are meant to be entertaining and informative, but are not "hard news."
- Feature structure can be more flexible than the inverted pyramid.
- Much of what is printed or broadcast is feature-type material.
- There are many types of features, depending on the subject matter.
- Feature leads are not necessarily summary in nature. Their purpose is to entice the reader or viewer to continue with the feature.
- Features should be fun to write and read, and are best learned by doing.

CHAPTER 10 – PHOTOGRAPHS

- Digital photography, image editing and e-mailing images is the way to go.
- Photography is a valuable and necessary skill to enhance your PR efforts.
- PR photography is a branch of photojournalism called "editorial photography."
- Photos should be clear, focused and information-rich. Forget "artsy" effects.
- Basic photographic equipment will serve for public relations work.
- Learning basic image editing – cropping, resizing, resampling, brightness and contrast changing, sharpening and noise reduction – will be enough to greatly improve your PR photo submittals.
- JPEG image format is best for nearly every type of image.
- Consider file compression for your e-mailed images.
- Learn the basics of good photography and know how to avoid the most common exposure errors.
- Know the legal aspects of photojournalism.
- Film-based photographic submittals still are accepted, but are a lot more work.

CHAPTER 11 – MEDIA KITS

- Contain a variety of information to help provide an overview of your organization.
- Should be updated regularly.
- Keep your media kit simple and inexpensive by producing easy-to-update, easy-to-print material that can be inserted into a binder.
- Can accompany a news release.
- Are useful for other purposes than just sending to the media: Kits can help sell products or services, just like advertising.

CHAPTER 12 – OTHER MEDIA-CONTACT METHODS

- Personal contact, such as telephone calls and face-to-face meetings, are accepted and effective ways to connect with journalists.
- News release and feature material can be placed via paid adverting, especially if the media does not act on a newsworthy PR submittal.
- Opportunities to contact the media and generate favorable PR occur constantly.
- Unless you're flush with a large public relations budget, video news releases are prohibitively expensive, of dubious value and quickly become outdated.
- Complaining about public relations placements and constantly calling to push a PR project do not work and are counterproductive.

CHAPTER 13 – MEDIA RELATIONS

- The media has a lot of power, and they know it.
- Cultivate a good relationship with the media that matter to you.
- Honesty, accuracy, responsiveness, fairness and gratitude work better than anger and stonewalling.
- Lies will be found out.

CHAPTER 14 – CRISIS MANAGEMENT

- Should be part of a public relations plan.
- Negative publicity can be long-lasting and even terminal to a business or organization. It should be dealt with quickly.
- Always stress the positive during a crisis.
- Brainstorm to determine how you are crisis-prone.
- Prepare a crisis communications plan in advance.
- Designate a single spokesperson.
- Make sure everyone in the organization knows their role in a crisis.
- Get to know local reporters.
- Learn to recognize the methods of reporters.
- Don't disregard the damage potential of rumors.
- Review the effectiveness of your PR crisis measures after the crisis is over.

CHAPTER 15 – LEGAL CONSIDERATIONS

- Involvement with the publishing or broadcast of information places public relations people under the same laws that govern journalists.
- A special body of laws protects and restrains journalists.
- Know the elements and defenses of libel.
- Truth is the ultimate defense for libel.
- Learn the concepts behind invasion of privacy in U.S. law.
- Recording conversations, meticulous proofreading, obtaining releases and clearing the contents of a story with those concerned are among the way to avoid libel and invasion of privacy problems.
- Find out if the states in which your conversation takes place are "one party" or "two party" consent states for the purposes of legal recording.
- Most reporter/informant shield laws are meaningless in practice.
- Copyright law now is very simple, due to the "Berne Convention."
- "Work for hire" usually entitles employers and clients to intellectual property.
- If your PR activities manage to provoke a lawsuit, get a lawyer.

CHAPTER 16 – MEASURING RESULTS

- Full-blown PR campaigns by agencies often involve surveys before, during and after the campaigns to determine problem areas, where changes are needed, and the effectiveness of the public-relations effort.

- Surveys are expensive and imprecise, but there are ways to determine if your PR activities are making a difference.

- Don't attempt to conduct a large-scale public opinion survey on your own.

- Keep your opinion research low-key, simple and unambiguous.

CHAPTER 17 – REFERENCE RESOURCES

- Keep your reference works within reach of your keyboard.

- Get both the AP Stylebook and Webster's New World College Dictionary.

- Develop your own local "style sheet" for names, preferred terms, industry jargon and easily misspelled words.

- Add your local style sheet entries to your word processor's spell checker.

CHAPTER 18 – STYLEBOOK QUIZZES

- A working knowledge of the AP Stylebook is critical to create professional public relations materials.

- Regular use of the Stylebook, even on correspondence, school homework and other non-PR writing will reinforce its conventions.

- The AP Stylebook is updated regularly, so have the latest edition and toss the previous one.

- The Stylebook quizzes included should be attempted with the book closed. These are the same kind of tests college journalism students must pass.

CHAPTER 20
ABOUT THIS BOOK

Michael R. Gearlds holds a journalism degree with honors from the University of Arizona and has worked as an editor, reporter, feature writer and photographer for newspapers, magazines, government agencies, advertising and public relations companies, mail-order retailers and the aerospace industry.

Since 1988, he has taught college courses and seminars in reporting, advertising and public relations, magazine and feature writing, photojournalism, digital photography and media studies.

He currently lives in North Idaho, where he has worked as a journalism teacher, reporter, magazine feature writer, political columnist and cartoonist. He continues to work in the public relations sector, fulfilling projects for businesses and organizations through his company, *North Star Public Relations*.

Do Your Own Public Relations! was born from his college business seminar of the same name, which presented the basics of creating and distributing news releases. Feedback from seminar participants showed there was a need for a straightforward guide that small businesses, organizations and individuals could use to produce affordable and effective public relations materials.

Since the first edition of this book in 1991, much has changed in the way public relations documents are created and distributed, specifically the Internet, e-mail and digital photography. Ever-more-powerful personal computers, software, printers, cameras and Internet capabilities and speed have made small office-based public relations even more feasible to virtually anyone.

Your comments are welcome: Praise, criticism, complaints, corrections and additions may be sent to:

NORTH STAR PRESS
P.O. Box 299
Hope, ID 83836

Do Your Own Public Relations! will be updated periodically as the media and technology evolve, and to reflect feedback from its valued readers.

NOTES

NOTES

NOTES

www.ingramcontent.com/pod-product-compliance
Lightning Source LLC
Chambersburg PA
CBHW081825280526
45789CB00007B/2348